Praise for
Breaking Free from a Malignant Manager

"Being in a job with a malignant manager is one of the worst professional experiences I have known. Cathy has coached me, several times, through bad managers. Cathy's book provides insightful ideas and tools to help you manage the situation and find the best way forward for you. It won't be easy, but this book will demonstrate that you are *not alone* and that you *will survive* this occupational challenge. It offers proven techniques and constructive action that you can take *today* to win back the control and confidence you need to survive a malignant manager."

—Philanthropic Executive*

*Names omitted to protect identities.

"This book is a lifeline for anyone suffering in silence, like I once did. I remember all too well how those days were filled with self-blame, stress, and anxiety. What you need are strategies to move forward, and you will find those here. The stories and quotes throughout the book also help you connect to the countless other people who have gone through—and survived—similar experiences. I'm now in a role where I'm valued and respected, and many of the strategies on these pages are the ones that helped me get here."

—Facilities & Operations Executive*

"I spent years questioning my worth under a manager who thrived on control and criticism. I wish I could have read this book at the time, because it would have saved me so much misery, and helped me realize that I wasn't alone. Cathy Alfandre's tone is calm, supportive, and encouraging, and her coping strategies are empowering. I highly recommend this book to anyone who is stuck in the nightmare of working for a malignant manager!"

—Former Marketing Executive*

"With more than 30 years of industry experience, I unfortunately had two particularly bad (aka "malignant") managers. I wish I had had this valuable resource! Cathy Alfandre deftly describes how to recognize, cope, and move forward from "malignant" managers and the stress they can induce. She provides many real-life examples of the workplace challenges and offers numerous solutions to not only navigate through them, but move onward and upward in your career and life. A practical, thoughtful read for any professional struggling with a difficult manager."

—Healthcare Executive*

Names omitted to protect identities.

"Unfortunately, no professional is immune from a bad manager. I experienced this phenomenon mid-career and the experience was disillusioning and disempowering. Thankfully, I worked with Cathy Alfandre who equipped me with strategies to manage the malignant manager and to chart my own professional future. She is the perfect professional to write this book, which provides actionable strategies for managing the emotional (and physical) toll that malignant management imposes. It is a real guide for reclaiming your professional agency and charting your own future free of the toll of malignant management."

—Higher Education Professor*

"For years, I internalized the distress of working under a malignant manager, and it ultimately broke my connection to a mission I had devoted my life to. Cathy's coaching helped me validate what I was going through, realign my self-worth with my career, and liberate myself from the weight of that toxic dynamic. Now that her ideas, guidance, and strategies are available in this book, anyone in a similar situation can benefit."

—Government Analyst*

"Having faced several malignant managers over my career, I know how easily your confidence can be shaken and your ambitions sidelined. This book not only normalizes these all-too-common experiences, but—with Cathy's caring and pragmatic guidance—helps you rediscover your strength and true worth. Her approach is honest and empathetic, giving you the clarity and tools needed to move forward and pursue the career you deserve."

—Finance Professional*

Names omitted to protect identities.

"As an HR leader, I've witnessed the profound impact that a destructive or misaligned manager can have on an employee's morale, mental health, and overall well-being. This book is a resource for anyone who feels overlooked, diminished, or under constant stress due to their manager's behavior, providing not only encouragement but also clear strategies to rebuild confidence and take purposeful steps forward. What makes this book especially valuable is its broad relevance—it speaks directly to employees at all levels, while also serving as an insightful resource for HR professionals and career coaches. With specific guidance and empowering insights, it shows readers that they have choices and that real, meaningful change is possible. I highly recommend it to anyone feeling stuck or unsupported in their work environment."

—Chief Human Resources Officer*

"In my therapy office, clients often discuss toxic managers at work, the place where many of us spend the majority of our waking hours. These difficult interactions destroy self-confidence, rob people of enthusiasm and potentially contribute to clinical levels of anxiety or depression. Drawing on her 20+ years as a career coach, Cathy Alfandre has written a compassionate and easy-to-read guide that validates these experiences and provides actionable tools to challenge counterproductive thoughts, communicate effectively, and strategize about next steps. I will strongly recommend this book to clients and other mental health providers."

—Judith Saltzberg, Ph.D.
Founding Fellow, Academy of Cognitive Therapy

Names omitted to protect identities.

"As a licensed clinician, I often meet clients when they are at some of the most difficult and upsetting times of their lives. When problems occur in the workplace, clients will usually attempt to reach out to their managers or supervisors for support. However, the manager or supervisor can sometimes be the cause of the difficult situation in the workplace. Cathy Alfandre's book examines some of the more common types of malignant or toxic managers, and then gives concrete and ready-to-use strategies to deal with the situation, from making the workplace more conducive to staying with that employer, all the way to preparing to leave and move on. I will recommend this book to my colleagues and any clients who are trying to figure out how to cope with a bad manager."

—Martin Brault, MS, AADC, LADC
Licensed Alcohol and Drug Counselor

"This is a truly remarkable book that can empower readers with skills and strategies to address their difficult situation rather than just seeing themselves as victims with limited options. It draws on real-world scenarios and offers specific suggestions to help readers reclaim their confidence. As a career coach and former HR director, I've seen firsthand how destructive some managers can be. Malignant managers are a regrettable reality of the workplace. The power of this book is to offer practical solutions to complex, but common situations. It is a must-read for anyone seeking to enhance their professional skills and deal successfully with challenging managers and circumstances."

—Mark Cohen
Career Coach and former Director of Human Resources

"As a Career Coach and former HR leader, I have too often seen how a malignant manager can strip an employee of their self-esteem and cause them to question their whole career. This book is a must read for anyone suffering in a harmful work environment. It offers support and hope, validates what feels like a lonely experience, and provides numerous strategies to survive and thrive again."

—Jeanne Knight
Career Coach and former Director of Human Resources

Breaking Free
from a
Malignant
Manager

Breaking Free
from a
Malignant Manager

STRATEGIES TO RECLAIM
YOUR CONFIDENCE & CAREER

CATHY ALFANDRE

PYP **Publish** Your Purpose

For permission requests, write to the publisher, addressed "Attention: Permissions Coordinator," at the address below.

Publish Your Purpose
141 Weston Street, #155
Hartford, CT 06141

PYP **Publish** Your Purpose

The opinions expressed by the Author are not necessarily those held by Publish Your Purpose.

Ordering Information: Quantity sales and special discounts are available on quantity purchases by corporations, associations, and others. For details, contact the author at cathy@cathyalfandre.com.

Edited by: Emily Ribeiro
Cover design: Nelly Murariu
Typeset by: Medlar Publishing Solutions Pvt Ltd., India

ISBN: 979-8-88797-194-0 (hardcover)
ISBN: 979-8-88797-193-3 (paperback)
ISBN: 979-8-88797-195-7 (ebook)
Library of Congress Control Number: 2025913065

First edition, November 2025.

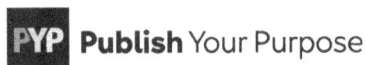

Publish Your Purpose is a hybrid publisher of non-fiction books. Our mission is to elevate the voices often excluded from traditional publishing. We intentionally seek out authors and storytellers with diverse backgrounds, life experiences, and unique perspectives to publish books that will make an impact in the world. Do you have a book idea you would like us to consider publishing? Please visit PublishYourPurpose.com for more information.

For Victor:
I carry you in my heart.

Contents

Introduction

YOU ARE NOT ALONE

When you hear the word "boss," does your heart start racing? Do you have a pit in your stomach? Do you feel nothing but dread?

I have been a professional career coach since 2003, and if there is one recurring theme across my conversations with hundreds of clients, it is this: Countless people are miserable at work because of the way they are managed. Their managers' behaviors have marred or ruined their self-esteem, sapped their energy, and sometimes damaged their physical health. Over thousands of hours of conversation, I recognize all too well the tones of exhaustion, anger, frustration, and even fear in these clients' voices. My heart aches when I hear it.

To be sure, there are many excellent managers out there, and there are numerous other reasons people change jobs and careers. But with astonishing frequency, I talk with professionals at all levels who have reached the point where their managers have made their working lives unbearable. When these clients reach out to me, our work together focuses on helping them get unstuck, regaining a sense of strength, navigating their situation at work, and, eventually, making a transition to a new role.

This book is for those of you who are like so many—too many— of my clients, usually suffering quietly, but truly suffering. *I want you to know that you are not alone.* I want you to know that you are not to blame for those frequent horrible feelings of confusion, dread, fear, sadness, anger, and hopelessness. If your physical and mental health have taken a hit, that's not because of something you did wrong. If you find yourself questioning everything about your skills and qualifications or even your career choice . . . those thoughts aren't your fault either. Over the course of months or years, the experience of dealing with an awful manager can stir up these kinds of damaging feelings and thoughts.

These managers, by the way, are everywhere. I have spoken with clients in the banking, consulting, elementary and secondary education, higher education, finance, government, healthcare, home care, media, non-profit, pharmaceutical, and tech sectors. They're in every function as well, including marketing, fundraising, sales, human resources, operations, finance, project management, legal, software engineering, facilities, and more. These managers—men and women, younger and older—can be found at all levels of the organization and sometimes at the very top.

From my perspective, these managers aren't just incompetent— they're malignant. In a non-medical sense, some definitions of malignant include: "disposed to cause suffering or distress . . . malicious . . . dangerous . . . harmful in influence or effect . . . injurious . . . having intense, often vicious, ill will . . ."[1] Even when we think of malignancy

---

[1] *The American College Dictionary* (Random House, 1962), 737; *Webster's Third New International Dictionary* (Merriam-Webster Incorporated: 1993), 1367.

in medical terms, such as "tending to produce deterioration . . . tending to spread . . . deadly,"[2] the description also holds true to a certain extent. These managers' behavior harms their teams and their organizations, creating a deadening effect on the culture that spreads to everyone in their orbit. While I am aware of only one client getting to the point of suicidal ideation, these managers can proverbially kill something inside—a sense of pride in work, feelings of self-worth, and even hope.

The behavior of malignant managers takes many forms. It's sadly easy to envision the abusive, demeaning, or hypercritical manager. We've seen them occasionally in popular culture—think Miranda Priestly in *The Devil Wears Prada* or Bill Lumbergh in *Office Space*, for example. Most of the time, when reporting to a manager like this, it's pretty clear that this manager is a problem. But there are other, sometimes subtler forms that these managers take, from behind-your-back conniving, to stealing credit for your work, to outright neglect. The quieter forms of malignancy can have a more insidious effect, and it might take longer to realize what's going on and how damaging the situation is. But every variety of malignant manager is a problem, and each one's impact is real and lasting.

"HOW DO I KNOW THAT I'M NOT THE PROBLEM?"

Now you may be wondering: how do I distinguish a manager who's simply pushing hard for great performance from one who's malignant? And how do I know that I'm not just overly sensitive to criticism

---

[2] *Merriam-Webster Dictionary*, "malignant," accessed February 25, 2025, https://www.merriam-webster.com/dictionary/malignant.

or just have unrealistic expectations of what my manager should be? There's a spectrum of behavior, for sure, and it's possible that a manager's push for performance could be mistaken as unduly harsh.

One angle to consider is whether your manager has multiple direct reports and you're the only one on the team who is unhappy. If others seem to be thriving and never seem to be the target of your manager's awful behavior, then it may be worthwhile to examine whether there's anything different or subpar about your performance. If so, then a good manager—one who is willing and eager to support you and help you learn—can work with you to address your performance gap. An honest self-examination and subsequent discussion with your manager should help to establish what's wrong and what steps can be taken to fix the issue(s).

But you can be sure that your manager is truly malignant if (1) their damaging behaviors are recurring or sustained over a period of at least three months, (2) you rarely or never feel encouraged, supported, developed, or engaged in your work, and (3) you have ongoing feelings of dread, fear, sadness, hopelessness, or worse at work. From my point of view, the purpose of people management is to cultivate the best possible performance from everyone on the team and to provide them with the feedback, resources, time, training, and environment that will allow them to achieve that level of performance. The feedback managers provide should be timely and thoughtful, including both positive and constructive insights into their direct reports' performance. Within a few months on any job, you should have received such feedback, guidance, and support to elevate your performance. Malignant managers do none or very little of this.

Consider one other point about malignancy: I don't think all malignant managers have malicious intent. Actually, I think very few of them do. But their cluelessness and/or unwillingness to self-examine, ask for feedback, and grow as a manager does not excuse their harmful behavior.

WHAT THIS BOOK AIMS TO DO

I'll begin by shining a light on the pernicious, often lasting impacts that malignant managers have on their employees. Perhaps you've noticed that these managers can distort your perception of your own skills or self-worth. Their behaviors can have a direct impact on your job performance, making it nearly impossible to do your best and steadily decimating your goodwill toward the organization. These managers can even affect day-to-day mental and physical health. I will share some of the common impacts in the next chapter, and I hope that you'll see how others' experiences are much like your own.

After that, I'll describe seven types of malignant managers—the ones I have seen again and again—with details to illuminate what their behaviors look like and how they are experienced by those unlucky enough to work for them. If you have a malignant manager, you may notice that yours fits one or more of the types.

I will then share a variety of strategies for coping with your malignant manager. Despite how hopeless you may feel at this moment, there are steps you can take to improve your situation, even if you feel stuck, unready, or unwilling to leave your job. Like many of my clients, you may not be in a position to quit, but that doesn't mean you just have to suffer.

If and when you *are* ready to leave, I'll offer some specific suggestions to help you work steadily toward an exit. Toward the end of the book, I'll provide strategies and tactics to avoid working for a malignant manager in the future and then close with a few notes on how to think about and learn from your awful experience once you have moved on.

Throughout the book, I will share quotes from my clients to illuminate what it feels and looks like to be (mis)treated by malignant managers and to show some specific examples of malignant behavior. It may be helpful to note that these clients have included individual contributors, managers, and executives. Some managers were forced into the position of protecting their own direct reports from the managers above them. You'll also hear about strategies and tactics my clients have used successfully to survive and thrive despite their managers. I'll present all of the stories and quotes anonymously, but they reflect the statements of real people across more than 60 interviews and conversations, and I am using their words with their permission. I hope their voices will inform, enlighten, and inspire you.

Ultimately, my purpose is to help you feel seen and heard and to renew your sense of hope, confidence, and strength on the job. We all deserve the opportunity to have fulfilling work lives and to use our skills and talents to create real impact. Life is too short to spend precious hours suffering at work.

WHAT THIS BOOK WON'T DO

As we all know from media stories, there are two egregious malignancies in many workplaces: racism and sexual harassment. While the effects of these behaviors can be crippling, this book will not delve into examples of these.

For one, such malignant behaviors violate the explicit workplace policies developed by nearly every organization (at least in the United States), so they are reportable and (theoretically) punishable by the organization and in courts of law. The malignancies addressed in this book are less clear-cut violations of any law but are still very tricky to navigate and address.

Second, while many have no doubt experienced discrimination and harassment, these issues have not been the focus of the coaching work I have done with most of my clients. I feel that I can best represent and shine a light on the situations that reflect what my clients have told me about their malignant managers and difficult workplaces. I will provide some resources at the end of this book on where to turn for legal support if you are experiencing racism or sexual harassment at work.

This book also will not propose ways to be a better manager. There are countless excellent books, consultants, and training programs that specialize in best-practice management techniques, and I will offer just a small selection of these resources at the end of this book. Happily, many of my most effective executive and management-level clients have taken advantage of resources like these and invested time, money, and energy into learning how to manage well. Unfortunately, there are far too many who have not.

I realize that many of you who suffer or have suffered under a malignant manager may also have your own direct reports. Perhaps you wonder about your own gaps as a manager and are unsure if your approach to management is malignant, benign, or healthy. If you're a manager, and you suspect or worry that you may fit one or more of the categories of malignancy, this book may offer a window into these behaviors and their effects on those you manage. I applaud you for reading and hope that this book provides some preliminary ideas for learning and insight. But way beyond this book, I urge you to take action and make a commitment to change—for your own sake, and for the sake of the people and the organization around you.

The Devastating Impact
of Malignant Managers

If you work for a malignant manager, the daily experience on the job slowly settles into your mind—sometimes your body—and feels like a steady and increasingly agonizing drumbeat: Dread. Fear. Shame. Sadness. Anger. Resentment. Hopelessness. Sickness. Sleeplessness. Exhaustion. These are only some of the words that my clients have used to describe the feelings that accompany them every day.

Let's start with one example—a quote from a client who worked for the same malignant manager for years.

"I proposed a solution to a process flow problem at work, but he told me, 'things aren't done that way.' Later, my idea was actually implemented, saving the company millions. But was I recognized

for it? Nope. In fact, he took the credit. He treated me badly every single day, watching my projects like a hawk and never complimenting or showcasing my work. He tried to stop me from pursuing opportunities that were good for my career growth. As if all that weren't bad enough, he had no qualms about asking me and others on the team to work nights and weekends. He even asked me to cancel a vacation, making it clear that 'the right answer' was to agree to do so.

"Honestly, my sense of self-worth plummeted while I worked for him. Somehow, I let myself believe that it was my fault. He preyed on my insecurity and desire to do well and feel competent. I felt quite small and powerless. I started taking medication for acute anxiety. I lost a lot of sleep."

———————————

The hits to my client's confidence were real and profound and affected her in countless ways at work and at home, in the short-term and the long-term. For the rest of this chapter, I'll delve more into the various types of impacts that malignant managers have on their people, with more real-world testimonials.

Before getting into the different forms of negative impact, I do want to highlight that some of my clients have seemed more vulnerable to their malignant managers' behavior than others. I didn't want to compound their already painful experience by asking why they took it so hard, but I suspect a few reasons. Some placed significant weight on their work as a measure of their self-worth. A few had unfortunately worked for more than one terrible boss, and the recurring experience compounded their sense of distress. Some felt "stuck," even "trapped," in their current situation, and so their suffering had an extra layer of frustration and fear.

On the flip side, some of my clients have been able to see very clearly that the situation was not their fault. Some were sure they could find another job when they were ready, or they felt comfortable that if they had to quit and take a break from work, it wouldn't harm their future candidacy. Some had side jobs or businesses as a backup. A few had a measure of job security, so they could avoid or even confront their malignant manager without fear of getting fired. Others were just inherently strong, self-confident, and resilient, making it easier to distance themselves from their horrible treatment.

Regardless of how hard they took it in the moment, though, every one of my clients was affected in quite negative ways, and these experiences were etched upon their memories. Among the interviews I conducted, some recounted the behavior of managers from more than a decade ago quite vividly and painfully.

SELF-BLAME ("IT MUST BE MY FAULT")

One common response to a manager's malignant treatment is to assume that you must be doing something wrong. After all, the boss is responsible for assessing performance and gets to decide whether you're worthy of praise, encouragement, and support. If you're getting none of these, then it must be your fault, right? If only *you* were better somehow, all the issues would go away.

Unfortunately, direct reports often draw this erroneous conclusion, even when they *know* deep down that they're great at their jobs.

They're constantly second-guessing themselves, trying to figure out what they must have done wrong. When they have the benefit of distance from the situation, it's easier to see that they were absolutely not to blame. But I have heard language like this so often.

"I felt like he always looked at me and found me lacking. I kept thinking, 'I have to try harder. What did I do wrong?'"

"It took a long time before I stopped thinking, 'something's wrong with me.'"

A related kind of self-blame includes kicking oneself for simply being victimized. Especially if it happens more than once, employees can start to feel like there must be something that they are doing to attract such treatment or to put themselves in a position to be managed by someone so malignant.

"I felt ashamed that I let it happen to me."

"It's hard, when it's the second or third time, not to start blaming yourself."

It makes sense. It's hard to see the picture clearly when the person with power over your working life questions, criticizes, demeans, neglects, or abuses you. It's tempting to turn the lens inward . . . but let me assure you: It's not your fault.

PAINFUL HITS TO SELF-CONFIDENCE ("MAYBE I'M NO GOOD AT THIS WORK")

A related effect of malignant treatment is the loss of confidence at work. If your experience is constant critique or micromanagement, or the absence of feedback, recognition, and encouragement, it eventually becomes hard to know whether your output or skills are strong. Those who are new to their careers may be especially prone to self-doubt, but even those with years or decades of experience can develop a distorted self-perception. The longer the malignant treatment continues, the more you feel beaten down and incompetent.

"My self-confidence took a huge hit. Luckily, I knew I had a history of being successful in the workplace. If I hadn't had that, I can't imagine how devastating that would have been. Even so, it drained my soul. I felt like a husk."

"That experience affected me emotionally in a bad way. He knocked me off my stool. I couldn't sustain confidence in myself. He knocked me down a few notches. And I let him."

Sometimes the negative self-perception starts to generalize beyond the current role and situation, and you start to question not only your current performance but your career choice overall. It's like the experience with the current manager warps the entire picture of all that you have done to build a career to this point.

"I worked hard and worked my way up. And then I get to this job . . . I was demoralized. I started to second-guess my abilities. What's wrong with me? Why am I not understanding?"

"I felt completely incompetent and incapable, and completely forgot about the positive things I accomplished in this position as well as in all of my other roles. It was a dark, hopeless place."

These persistent thoughts are damaging. If you're spending 40-plus hours per week in a constant state of wondering whether you're cut out for the job, or even your whole career, it's very hard to feel anything but sadness, hopelessness, or worse. You might even start asking yourself questions like: Do I need to look for another line of work at this age? What kind of job am I even suited for? What if no one will hire me?

FEAR ("WHAT'S COMING NEXT?")

As we will see in more detail in the next chapter, some managers behave terribly all the time: They yell, humiliate, and abuse their staff members, or talk behind their backs constantly. Other managers are more erratic, and there's nothing like erratic behavior to make someone feel unsafe. You come in or log on each day, tiptoeing around, not knowing which version of your boss you'll encounter.

When facing this kind of manager, you might have a persistent, nagging pit in your stomach, filled only with fear and worry. Perhaps you sit on pins and needles wondering if the phone will ring, or an email or instant message will come in with a nasty critique.

"While I used to look forward to his texts, emails, and calls, I found myself dreading them. The sound of my phone notifications made my stomach turn because it could have been him reaching out."

"She had created an entire culture based on fear. I was so anxious all the time. It was such a relief when I could work from home. Whenever I had to go into the office, I felt like I had to wear armor."

"I hated him and was terrified of him, too. Even when [they were doing an investigation and] I got called by counsel, I was terrified to tell the truth. I thought he would do something to destroy me."

Fears of retaliation or losing your job are also very real. Many of my clients are primary or sole breadwinners in their families and are not in a position to risk saying something either to their boss or to other powers that be, such as their boss's boss or HR. Or perhaps the job offers benefits that feel too important to lose. More than one client gained employment through a work visa; losing that job would mean having to leave the country. Malignant managers may specifically take advantage of this dependency, getting away with their horrible behaviors with impunity.

"I carried the benefits and my husband was self-employed. I would have quit in a heartbeat if not for the benefits."

"I allowed myself to be vulnerable because my husband was unemployed and I had children. I took the job because it was closer to

home and didn't require me to be on the road. I didn't want to be a mother who was always away. I wanted to be near them and be able to manage their needs."

"She made me nervous going into meetings because she would want things so quickly and question why I didn't have all the answers to everything. She was scary. I was on a working visa and couldn't jeopardize my job and ability to stay in the US. I didn't have the ability to speak up or go to her boss."

——————

No one should experience chronic fear and stress at work. They are not in the job description! Even worse, chronic stress over weeks and months is associated with high cortisol levels, which according to the Cleveland Clinic, can lead to inflammation and a host of mental and physical health problems, from anxiety to weight gain to heart disease.[3] More on those effects in a moment.

DETERIORATING PERFORMANCE ("WHY SHOULD I CARE?")

Most managers, good and bad, are focused on getting the best productivity and performance out of their staff. There's work to do and they're eager to get it done, usually quickly and with the highest level of quality. Ironically, the behavior of troubling managers will

---

[3]"Yes, There Is Such a Thing as Stress Sickness," The Cleveland Clinic, December 1, 2023, https://health.clevelandclinic.org/what-happens-when-your-immune-system-gets-stressed-out.

sometimes push their staff to "check out" mentally, sometimes doing the minimum to get by. Their resentment or anger about the situation leads them to disengage and withdraw their best efforts. They aim to care less as a means of preserving their dignity, energy, and even their sense of self. The thinking goes: "If my manager treats me this badly, why should I give my best in return?"

"It seemed like no matter what I did, she would keep behaving that way. It was a sinking feeling. Eventually I had no desire to go to work. I figured: 'Let them push me out so I can get a nice severance.'"

"It got to the point where I wasn't even behaving like myself. I decided I couldn't battle. So I just listened, didn't open my mouth, didn't say anything. I shut down."

"At first I was frustrated and confused. But then I was just demotivated. I let go. It wasn't worth it."

Interestingly, sometimes the work doesn't suffer at all. Staff members may put in extra effort to do the best possible job in the hopes of staving off the manager's critiques and harsh treatment. They may also continue to believe in the organization's mission and/or want to continue providing great service to its customers. In these cases, the impact is less on the work itself and more on the employees' internal stress levels.

Often, it's a combination of "checking out" while still trying to do one's best. Part of the mind wants to do well, stay focused on the important work at hand, and deliver with the work ethic and quality that meet the highest standards. At the same time, part of the mind is trying not to care too much, not to be too invested in the organization and the work, and not to attach too much weight to the job.

"I committed to myself that I'd try to do the best possible job so she'd have nothing to criticize, but part of me was always dreaming about how to get out of the situation. I recently looked back at a project I was working on and noticed I had missed an important step, and I know it was because I was distracted. I have to redouble my effort to stay focused!"

DETERIORATING GOODWILL TOWARD THE ORGANIZATION ("THIS COMPANY DOESN'T DESERVE THE BEST OF ME")

A close cousin of declining performance is a growing disinterest in doing your best for the organization itself. I have heard many clients over the years become cynical and disengaged, especially if the malignant manager's behavior is out of sync with the overall stated values and culture of the company. They see the organization doing nothing about their manager's hideous behavior and feel misled or even deceived. They see that the company places value on the results that the manager generates, but little to no value on how they achieve those results and the impact their methods have on the people underneath them.

"I kept thinking: 'why don't they fire him?' It was so egregious and bred so much ill will. It brought everyone's morale down. We all couldn't help thinking: 'why bother?'"

"She just got away with so much. It made me so bitter and angry. As long as she was performing and making money, they didn't care. I had and still have no goodwill toward the organization."

"People were always talking about the importance of our culture. But the culture was horseshit. At the end of the day, you're just a number."

So many questions inevitably come to mind, and so much anger bubbles up: How do they get away with it? Why doesn't anyone notice? Why doesn't anyone support me? It's hard to remain emotionally connected to an organization that you feel has failed you.

MENTAL AND PHYSICAL HEALTH IMPACTS ("I FEEL SICK")

The sustained stress of dealing with a malignant manager takes a toll on the mind and body. While I'm not a licensed psychologist, I have had many clients who exhibited signs or told me of their diagnoses of anxiety and depression. As I mentioned earlier, one client even expressed thoughts of suicide. Luckily, she was working with a skilled therapist who was able to help her process these feelings and move forward without self-harm. Even if the mental health impacts stop short of clinical diagnoses, they're very real.

"When you're in it, it feels like you're drowning. It's just darkness all around. You're in a box and there's nowhere to go. It's a bad, bad feeling. It was very debilitating."

Quite a few of my clients have had severe impacts on their physical health as well, including sleeplessness, chronic illness, weight gain, and weight loss. It's not too surprising, since numerous studies and organizations like the Mayo Clinic have shown the negative impacts of stress on physical health.[4] One client, for example, was diagnosed with Type 2 diabetes while working for a malignant manager. She felt that the stress on the job, combined with poor diet—due to long hours, she frequently went for quick and unhealthy meals—led directly to this condition. Indeed, since leaving the job, her health has improved significantly. Another client was so mistreated by his boss that he couldn't eat and ended up losing 30 pounds in three months! Similarly, upon escape from his malignant manager, his appetite slowly returned to normal.

While other clients' experiences were perhaps less dramatic, the mental and physical health impacts were still painful and lasting.

"I gained a lot of weight and my health suffered."

"While I was working for her, it really affected my sleep. I had to use the Calm app to settle down. The anxiety was overwhelming."

---

[4]"Chronic stress puts your health at risk," Mayo Clinic, August 1, 2023, https://www.mayoclinic.org/healthy-lifestyle/stress-management/in-depth/stress/art-20046037.

"I was exhausted mentally and frequently couldn't sleep. I had all the classic depression symptoms."

———————

Overall, if you take a step back and think about these examples for even a few moments, it doesn't take long to realize just how wrong these situations are. No one should get sick because of their experience at work!

IMPACT ON FINDING A NEW JOB ("HOW WILL I EVER EXPLAIN WHY I LEFT?")

The emotional experience of dealing with a malignant manager can sometimes affect a person's ability to find a new position somewhere else. If you consider a job interview, for example, one of your main goals as a candidate is to present your skills and readiness to do the job. But if your self-esteem has taken a hit and you've been questioning whether you're even cut out for the work anymore, how are you supposed to put your best foot forward?

———————

"When I finally started interviewing for new jobs, I realized my confidence was shot. I gave weak or veiled answers. I was so nervous. My body language must have been horrible. I actually ended up in another bad situation; I never would have accepted that next job if I hadn't been in a dark place."

———————

And if one of your main goals is to escape your horrible manager, how do you answer without sounding negative when the interviewer asks why you want to leave your job?

"I know you're not supposed to say anything bad about your current employer. But I know I kept sounding guarded and like I was hiding something. I didn't even look healthy. No wonder I had trouble getting to the next round."

Even before getting to an interview, you need to embark on typical job search activities—networking, for example, as well as looking and applying for jobs online. But if your boss has constantly critiqued or harangued or neglected you, how can you pull together a confident "pitch" about what you're looking for? If your recent experience has made you unsure what you even bring to the table anymore, how do you reach out to your contacts with poise? If you doubt your competence, job postings start to look like long lists of things you're no longer sure you can do. Pitfalls are everywhere, reinforcing a sense of feeling hopeless and stuck.

FAMILY IMPACTS
("I CAN'T GET AWAY FROM IT")

While naturally everyone tries to compartmentalize and create boundaries between work and home life, it's not always possible to do so—understandably. If you feel beaten down, afraid, angry, hopeless, or even sick for 40–60 hours or more per week . . . you can only keep these feelings to yourself for so long. It's natural to share with your partner, family members, and friends as you try to get the support you're not receiving at work, and to seek ideas and strategies to manage the situation.

But then, guilt arrives too—feeling terrible about "dumping" on your family and friends and tainting your personal life and "off" time with what's going on at work. As if you didn't feel bad enough about everything happening on the job! Despite their good intentions and love for you, your family and friends may also not be sure how to advise you, especially if the issues at work persist for a while (which they usually do). So your loved ones feel frustrated and uncertain, which only makes you feel more hopeless and regret burdening them.

"A shitty manager affects everyone in the orbit of their direct report. I had less patience for my kids and spent less time with them. My kids frequently complained: 'You don't love us. All you do is work.' Even when I wasn't working, I was so exhausted that I didn't want to do anything. I was so tired, I didn't even want to go for a walk. It affected my husband too. In a lot of ways, he was a single parent. I retreated from everybody. I didn't have time or desire to reach out to friends. I also didn't want them to ask, 'How's work?' It had a pervasive effect on my life and those around me."

"I realized my constant venting and anger and sadness about my boss was starting to affect my family time. I had to consciously say to myself every day: 'No talk about work tonight—this needs to be a boss-free zone.'"

While it's likely that your family members and friends don't feel that you are burdening them, there's no doubt that they are affected.

They don't want to see you stressed or hurt, and they do wish that you could fully be with them in your life outside of work. In this sense, the behavior of horrible managers has effects that reverberate beyond their direct reports—another sign of their malignancy as their impact spreads in harmful ways.

THE VICIOUS CYCLE

Another insidious aspect of malignant behavior is that the negative impacts beget more malignant behavior. For example, one client was frequently criticized for her communication skills. Instead of being coached and given opportunities to build her skills and shine, she was placed in high-pressure, high-stakes presentation situations. The fear of harsh critiques and demeaning comments led her to place significant pressure on herself to perform well. This led to sleepless nights and lots of worry, which resulted in occasional mistakes in her communications . . . which only led to further harsh critiques.

———

"At the time I wasn't aware, but I just started doing things with less confidence. It felt like a no-win situation. Of course, I see now that she put me into that situation. It was only after I left that I could see it."

———

The malignant behavior also leads to imperfect decision making, which unfortunately elicits more mistreatment.

"Because I was worrying all the time, I didn't feel confident enough to say we needed more help. I assumed he would think I was incompetent. I didn't advocate for myself when I should have. I tried to make up for it by working harder. But of course, that wasn't enough, and our team's output suffered."

It's hard to break out of this kind of cycle when you're feeling afraid, beaten down, confused, ill, or all of the above. You make poor decisions or second-guess yourself constantly. You're not in an optimal place to perform well or attempt to change your manager's perspective about you. Your malignant manager's critiques and opinions become self-fulfilling prophecies. The downward spiral feels inevitable and sickening.

LINGERING EFFECTS

All of these different effects don't simply vanish once you escape a malignant manager. Tongue in cheek, a client once shared: "It took me a while to get past the PTSD." But there's a serious nugget of truth there. Many of the clients I interviewed about their experiences had very vivid memories and became quite emotional, months or even years later.

"To this day if I hear the ringtone I had for him, it makes me nauseous. It takes the air out of the room."

"It's a terrible feeling, even years later. I'm feeling it now talking with you about those days."

"Even now, six years later, my heart's pounding and I'm worked up."

———————

Because the scars from these experiences can take time to heal, you may continue to have a distorted self-perception and behave in dysfunctional ways even after you move to a new job or company, affecting your ability to learn, grow, communicate, and even perform. While all of my clients were eventually able to move on and thrive, some had to go through an extended process of recovery. The harm that malignant managers inflict is real and often lasting.

While I've tried to tease apart the various impacts that malignant managers have on their direct reports, the unfortunate reality is that most people experience multiple impacts simultaneously, with compounding effects. My client who was yelled at and demeaned regularly felt a combination of self-blame, fear, illness, and (naturally) declining goodwill toward the organization. Another client who got no feedback and was essentially ignored felt angry, confused, and withdrawn, and his performance suffered. A third—who had to deal with a highly erratic manager—blamed herself, often felt scared and unsafe, and her family was affected by her ordeal.

In the next chapter, we'll take a look at some of these managers—the ones wreaking such damage—to better understand the malignancies that so many employees have to face. As we'll see, there are a lot of these managers out there. It's not you.

KEY TAKEAWAYS

1. Malignant managers can have a wide range of devastating impacts on those they manage, including self-blame, damage to self-confidence, chronic fear and worry, poor job performance, diminished goodwill toward the organization, deteriorating mental or physical health, and difficulties finding a new job.
2. The effects of malignant management often bleed into family life and other life outside work as well.
3. Don't be surprised if you experience more than one of these effects. They can combine and intensify your sense of feeling stuck and helpless.
4. These effects can settle in your mind and body, and it may take a while to uproot them and recover. (But you will!)

This Is What Malignancy Looks Like

I've heard many malignant manager stories over the years, and they pain me every time. These stories usually come out in my first conversation with a client, when they tell me that their manager has made their job intolerable. Their experiences go *way* beyond simple complaints about work and being bossed around. Their struggle is not about those moments that virtually everyone has, when their job is exhausting, or stressful, or unsatisfying, or annoying, or when their boss acts in a way that's off-putting or insensitive. After all, every manager has a bad day (or more than one). We can cope with that.

The distinction between a typically annoying manager and a truly malignant one is the sustained nature of the behavior and the harmful effects. Malignant managers' direct reports experience these behaviors day in and day out, week in and week out. There might be moments of benign management where employees might even start to get their hopes up that things are changing, but without fail, the behavior slides back to its normal malignant pattern.

Horrible managers take many forms. Sometimes the hideousness and harm are obvious—yelling, public embarrassment, micromanagement—and suffering under one of these kinds of managers is agony. Other malignancies are more subtle or hidden from public view—taking credit for others' work, talking behind others' backs, or neglecting the people they manage. Whether overt or camouflaged, the recurring behaviors are damaging to their direct reports, causing the types of devastating effects we saw in the last chapter, from self-blame, fear, and lower self-esteem to declining performance and deteriorating physical health.

Some of you reading this book already know you have a malignant manager. I'm guessing that there are others who wonder whether their manager fits the bill. Especially if you have a manager who's not a screamer, you might doubt at times whether they're truly malignant. So, ask yourself the following questions about the warning signs of malignant management:

1. Are your manager's damaging behaviors recurring or sustained over a period of at least three months? In other words, does your experience with them feel consistently harmful to you?
2. Do you rarely or never feel encouraged, supported, developed, or engaged in your work?
3. Do you have ongoing feelings of dread, fear, sadness, hopelessness, or worse at work?
4. Do you feel like your job and work environment are quashing your talents and energy?
5. Is your performance at work, and/or your mental health, and/or your physical health suffering?

If you found yourself answering yes to some or most of these, your manager is indeed malignant, and it's not likely to get any better.

As I've worked with hundreds of clients over the years who have been affected by malignant managers, I've noticed seven distinct types, which I'll describe in detail below. It may also be helpful to note here that some managers exhibit a mixture of malignant behaviors on different days or even on the same day. So don't be surprised if you recognize more than one of these types in *your* manager. Some managers are hard to characterize. In the next chapter, I'll share some possible strategies for dealing with the different types of managers. If your manager exhibits multiple types, your strategies may need to shift accordingly.

"WHY ARE THEY LIKE THIS?"

Before diving into the different types of malignant managers, I'd like to tackle a few questions I sometimes hear my clients ask: "Why is my manager treating me like this? She wouldn't want to be treated this way! Can't she see that? Can't she put herself in my shoes?"

I wish there were a good explanation. It does seem rather obvious from my perspective that respect, kindness, and encouragement are basic table stakes in the workplace. Considering that we spend so many hours on the job, it makes sense (to me) that everyone would want as positive and collegial a workplace as possible. Solid work performance and goal attainment are important, of course, but we don't need to treat people poorly to achieve results. In fact, countless clients have told me about excellent managers they've had and how they were never more engaged, never worked harder, and never performed better than they did for those positive role models.

A classic and likely reason for some malignant management could be as simple as the Peter Principle. In a nutshell, this principle states that a person who is competent at their job will likely be promoted to a position that requires different skills.[5] If they don't have the skills, they will be incompetent at this new level. Maybe you've seen it: A staff member is outstanding in their technical or functional area, and the company wants to promote them to recognize their performance. But just because they're strong technically, that doesn't mean they will naturally be effective at managing other people in technical roles! A high-performing individual contributor will not automatically become a high-performing manager. People often become managers without ever having been trained on how to manage, let alone how to manage well. They're clueless and choose to behave in ways that they *think* managers should behave. As it turns out, this cluelessness is sometimes far from benign.

Another explanation could be the workplace culture. If an organization does not evaluate, measure, reward, or otherwise hold managers accountable for their team's engagement and development, managers may choose to ignore these responsibilities. Or, even worse, some industries and companies create a pressure cooker environment where everything runs on tight timelines, client demands, and unrealistic targets. As one client described his industry: "It was filled with hyper-aggressive people with questionable morals because the environment was very, very competitive." The pressure to perform at all costs is seemingly baked into the organizational DNA. People get fired frequently, so there's a constant undercurrent of threat and fear. The harsh treatment typically starts from the very top.

---

[5]Laurence J. Peter and Raymond Hull, *The Peter Principle: Why Things Always Go Wrong* (William Morrow and Company, 1969).

Each manager's model is their own malignant manager, and the pro-verbial shit rolls downhill.

Often, these horrible managers are protected in some way by powerful players in the organization, such as top executives or boards who personally believe in someone's leadership or their track record of results. Sometimes they're a close friend of one of the organization's top executives, hand-picked and placed in their role. I'll often hear that managers in this situation master the skills of "kissing up and kicking down." They have a way of ingratiating themselves to the executives above them and finding ways to look really good. In these situations, you couldn't possibly go over their heads because the higher-ups are firmly in their corner.

But I've also seen that malignant managers can surface even when the overall organizational culture is positive and supportive. These situations are perplexing and you'll be tempted to speculate. Maybe they had horrible managers in past organizations and don't know how to act otherwise? Maybe they grew up in a toxic environment and have never had a role model for empathy and kindness, so this behavior is normal to them? Maybe they were a bully or mean girl and can't move past it? Maybe they are deeply insecure, afraid that if they don't act this way, they will somehow fail? Maybe they have no life outside of work, so the internal pressure to succeed at work distorts their behavior?

At the worst end of the spectrum, some of these managers may just be using their position of power to abuse those who report to them. They come to believe that their pursuit of results and recognition is all that matters and have no qualms or concerns about who they step on or how they treat those around them. Their behavior may mimic those of classic abusers—using coercion, threats, intimidation, blame, humiliation, and more to control those they manage and keep them feeling trapped in their roles.

A malignant manager's behavior is a puzzle that we want to solve, as if knowing the reason will somehow lead to a solution, or at least make things better. But you may not ever get to the bottom of it. Even if you do, it may not improve anything. **Knowing the reasons for a malignant manager's behavior will never justify it.**

Numerous examples will follow in the coming pages of the seven different types of malignant managers. As you'll see from the client experiences that I share along the way, there's no reasonable explanation or excuse for their behavior.

THE HUMILIATOR

Probably the most egregious type of malignant manager is the one who can't control his or her anger. They seem to have no trouble lashing out, insulting, and even verbally abusing you on a regular basis. There's nothing subtle about their behavior—it's frightening to be on the receiving end. You feel constantly unsafe. They've created an environment of fear and stress that is almost palpable. You always feel like something's coming and you're walking on pins and needles, trying to prepare yourself for the next explosion, jab, or insult.

Take one of my clients, for example. He took a new job working for someone he had known previously as a friend. Things started off well, but after a couple of months he noticed a shift and then the situation turned ugly.

"I took regular verbal beatings mixed in with an occasional 'coaching' session where he would be encouraging and helpful. I was insulted regularly in front of others or just one-on-one.

There were video calls where spit was flying from his mouth in anger. He even took a few swipes at the screen like he was trying to slap me across the face! On one of the calls, another colleague witnessed some of the anger toward me. When the colleague and I spoke about it later, he said: 'You know our boss always needs a villain.' I guess it was my turn."

―――――――――――

That feeling of being singled out and scapegoated is a theme I've heard from a number of clients. You can't always see how your manager is treating others, and it can seem very personal and targeted. It may actually be that you're alone in the crosshairs for a time before they move on to the next target. They need someone to blame for whatever is going wrong in the department, or in the business, or just that day. In these moments, the abusive or bullying behavior is very pointed and painful, and you can do nothing about it. Another client experienced something like this.

―――――――――――

"Her 'favorite children' could do no wrong, but there was always a scapegoat, and for a while that was me. She would shout at me and others in the middle of the hallway, anywhere. If I forgot to share a detail about a project with her, she would jump down my throat. If I caught a minor error, I was sure I'd be fired instead of appreciated. I started making all of my decisions in a defensive mode. I over-analyzed, just to avoid her potential harsh critique or public dressing down. At that time, I could have done that job blindfolded, but I kept asking myself: 'What am I doing wrong?'"

―――――――――――

Of course, sometimes you're not the scapegoat; someone else is. But the malignant behavior hurts you too—right in your gut—even when it's not directed at you. Picture this scene, for example: You're in a team or client meeting, and your manager publicly berates or humiliates another member of the team. They criticize her with anger and nastiness for something she did or didn't do. Here's a slightly more subtle form of humiliation: They ask your team member to report on the status of a project, even though they know it isn't done yet. Whatever your team member's mistake, large or small, they don't deserve this treatment and you know it. You're sick to your stomach. *Super* uncomfortable. You feel terrible for your teammate, and you're thinking: "How can he do this?" All those thoughts and feelings you're having? Those are spot on. There's no place for this kind of public shaming. It's wrong, but they're going to do it again. You also know that it could easily be you next time. One client described it as a kind of Russian roulette—you never knew when you were going to be the victim.

Perhaps the most painful situations are those where abusive and demeaning language is directed in a *very* personal way. In these cases, the managers somehow feel it is ok to try to cut their people down with a withering, cruel attack. It's hard to shake these off. Take this story, for example:

———————————

"The worst situation was when I went in to present a business plan. He was disengaged, looking at his computer. A lot of hard work went into it. When I finished, he said: 'Seems great but people would take you more seriously if you didn't have a Southern accent and lost 30 pounds.' It was like a slap in the face! It dawned on me then why no one else was in the room; it would have been a he-said-she-said kind of situation. I looked at him and said,

'You're serious, aren't you?' And he said, 'Of course I'm serious, how do you think our clients will take you seriously?' I had consistently demonstrated top performance, been promoted multiple times, and won tons of awards. None of that seemed to matter; he was determined to cut me down."

———————

There is literally no justification for this kind of treatment, and it's happening behind closed doors every day. While some abusive behaviors are right out in the open—in the hallway, on Zoom team calls, in meetings—others are happening in one-on-one meetings where you're basically cornered and have to take the insults and abuse. It's terrifying. And the feeling of helplessness is paralyzing.

The Humiliator type of malignant manager is perhaps the one we can all (unfortunately) imagine because we see examples in popular culture. Friends and family members tend to complain about them vociferously and share examples of their horrible behavior. But there are other types as well, and we'll take a look at them in the coming pages.

THE HYPER-CONTROLLER

Some malignant managers' daily, incessant practice is to find ways to control, comment on, and criticize their direct reports' work. With this type of manager, you quickly come to see that they can never be satisfied. Your work will never be good enough. Everything from major projects to email content is fair game. It will feel like the critiques keep piling up. Eventually you sense that there will be no way to get on this person's good side or do anything right. Their opinion of you seems cemented and unsalvageable. The inner voice that says, "maybe I really stink at this work," will start talking to you.

———————

"A new manager started and immediately started criticizing my work. He didn't help me improve in any way. He just pointed out what was wrong, even the tiniest little mistake like word choice in an email, and documented it. I had been in the role for three years and was really enjoying it. But within a couple of months of his arrival, I found myself second-guessing my entire career direction."

———————

Luckily, some don't lose faith in their abilities, but they do feel completely stymied by managers like this. For example, another client said:

———————

"Barely a day went by that she didn't find something to criticize— something I did, didn't do, how I phrased something. I became scared to say anything! Which doesn't work as a sales rep. She literally undermined my ability to do my job. When you're scared to open your mouth, you can't do your job anymore."

———————

Often, these non-stop criticizers are micromanagers who want to oversee, have a hand in, and comment on what seems like everything their direct reports do. There's no trust in their people's skills. They may check daily on what their direct reports are doing. They allow little or no autonomy in completing projects, communicating with colleagues and clients, or sometimes even managing their daily schedule. Direct reports can't proceed without reviews and approvals, so their productivity slows.

———

"I was shocked at how he saw us. He would take over my job responsibilities, or my team's, without telling us; he would do the work and then present it to us! He was also a fanatic about how things should look. He would change a single word in a document. He was constantly focusing on minutiae. He was intent on doing things his way; he literally couldn't give up the reins and had no vision that it might be ok to do things a different way. Maybe the worst was that he would save files where I didn't have access to them. He literally hindered my performance because I was responsible for these things. I had to go to him to ask for and get access. He had zero trust in me or any of us. It was so insulting."

———

Now you may be thinking: Don't managers have the right to oversee the quality of their direct reports' work? Shouldn't they carefully manage and critique performance that's less than optimal? And the short answer is yes, of course they should be involved and take ownership for the outputs of their team.

But there's a big distinction between management and malignant management. The benign (or better) manager may carefully oversee the work briefly, such as when the person is recently hired or promoted, providing guidance until it's time to pass the reins. Early on in a new hire's role, the manager may also offer more frequent feedback to course-correct anything that's not quite on point.

Malignant managers never take into account the ability of their direct reports to do the work nor their depth of experience. It doesn't even matter if their direct reports are senior level with a long track record of success in the role. Their executive-level boss still insists on overseeing and controlling the details and won't let go.

In addition, these managers offer little or no coaching and support; they will spend lots of time telling you what's wrong but invest little in helping you get better. They will take time away from their own jobs to micromanage others' jobs but see no point in empowering their direct reports to do the job well. They leave their people insulted, demoralized, and frustrated.

THE ROLLERCOASTER

Some managers are just plain unpredictable, and it's this unpredictability that is so malignant. On any given day, you have no idea what to expect! Some days, they're harsh and explosive. Some days they're benign, or even, dare I say, "nice." One day, they micromanage and critique everything you do. Another day, they tell you you're doing a great job. You feel that you have to prepare mentally for your day and how your manager might treat you, but you can't. This means that whatever strategies you might use to make your work experience more palatable just might turn out to be fruitless. The stress and fear of trying to deal with such an inconsistent and challenging person really piles up. On our first meeting, one client said about her manager:

"She is very erratic and inconsistent. She's famous for saying, 'This is what we should do,' and then the next day spinning around

and saying, 'Why would you do it this way?' She also comes out of nowhere like an aggressive whirling dervish. This has been such a hit to my confidence these last four years. I feel like I want to crawl in a hole. Other people have left and HR has told me they've seen the issues, but nothing has really been done. They gave her a coach, but she mocks it, saying that she has to go meet with her 'charm school teacher.'"

Perhaps unsurprisingly, the people who are forced to deal with this kind of manager are high performers. They do get positive feedback on the good days! So they are particularly confused when they're on the receiving end of outbursts. For example, another client said:

"I was afraid. I didn't know what to expect on any given day. One day I was appreciated for trying new things, but then later he started ripping me apart. I never knew when I was going to get reamed out. Overall, I got positive and actionable feedback during my annual reviews. But other times, he would just yell at me. Of course, I could improve some things but there was never anything that was a meaningful problem. I knew a lot of the problem was him. I knew I was doing a good job, but I still questioned my whole career. It was so, so damaging."

It isn't much of a stretch to realize that erratic managers are pretty emotionally unstable. It's impossible to know their emotional temperature in advance on any particular day, so you have to adapt your own actions according to your best assessment. Honestly, it shouldn't be part of your job description to have to do an emotional analysis of your boss each morning . . . . But that's what direct reports of these managers have to do.

——————

"After we agreed I'd do something, I would follow up with an email and ask her to confirm but get no response. Then I would act on it, and she would say, 'Why are you doing this? Who told you that you could do this?' Or she would tell me to reach out to others in a similar role and gather ideas from them. But then every idea I brought, she shot down immediately without a moment's thought—unless she was in a good mood. I had to figure out what mood she was in and wait until then to ask for something. I was dealing with purely emotional decision making."

——————

With these managers, you're always on edge, trying to prepare yourself for what may come, but never feeling very prepared. You're anxious and you dread work because you feel unsafe and on guard. The negative impacts on your self-perception and your mental health are virtually unavoidable.

THE CONNIVER

A close cousin of the prior types of malignant managers is the one who tells you "in confidence" what someone else is doing wrong. They seem to value you and you may feel that you've made it to the inner circle as a trusted team member and recognized high performer. But as they trash-talk others, it also feels uncomfortable—like childish gossip—and unfair because the people being critiqued can't defend themselves. That discomfort you feel only grows as the manager continues to talk behind others' backs. As one client put it, "I started to feel gross hearing these things about others, somehow complicit in this awful behavior."

In fact, sometimes it seems like you have no choice but to play along in order to get whatever information, resources, or other support you need. It's like there's an unwritten expectation that you have to participate in this behavior to stay on your manager's good side. Here's how one client described it:

"She would call me into a meeting but she didn't want to talk about work or the team or our strategies. She would just want to bitch about another member of the team; she'd trash her for an hour! I would have to endure it, go along with it, and wait until she'd get to the end of the crap she wanted to say before I could ask for what I needed. And now I'm the person she's talking about. She just needs someone to hate—that's the fuel that keeps her going."

As this client experienced, it doesn't take long before you see that your manager is talking about *you* too, because that's the way they operate. It has a sinister effect as you realize (as does everyone around you) that there's a constant background hum of badmouthing in the organization. You can't unhear what has been said about your coworkers, and neither can they. No one knows what's really true. All they know for sure is that the workplace has been rendered toxic. Everyone in the group is actually being taught and encouraged to engage in this kind of behavior because that's the example being set by the manager. So you might walk into a room and everybody suddenly quiets down. You feel constantly on alert, wondering what is being said about you, and that's how everyone else feels as well.

"He is clearly talking about my performance with others. I feel undermined and unsafe. It's a high-tension job, and I can't do it without support. I'm very experienced, but now I feel like I have to double- and triple-check myself. My confidence is plummeting. People think I'm crazy for putting up with this."

Some managers use these "confidential" conversations not only to criticize others but also to try to get inside information about their direct reports' peers, effectively trying to turn them into spies. They'll ask questions like: "Who, specifically, is having trouble with the changes?" or, "What did they tell you about how their team is doing against the numbers?" They're putting you in an uncomfortable position, putting you on the spot and asking you to divulge information shared with you by others. You can't help but wonder if your boss will somehow retaliate against you if you don't reveal what you know. You didn't sign up for this!

Meanwhile, they're getting the inside dirt on you from others, and they might just rub it in your face when they feel like it. "Someone said this about you," or, "I heard from someone that you didn't handle that well." This is particularly sinister because these statements aren't accompanied by a collaborative discussion with your boss about what happened from your perspective, specific insights into what may have gone wrong (if it did), nor specific coaching or feedback on how to improve. You're only left with the sense of a cloud over your head, like this:

———————————

"When he would regularly tell me that 'someone said this,' it was devastating. In every meeting, I feared that someone or some people would go and provide negative feedback to my boss. I was worried all the time; it was so detrimental. I was trying to grow and contribute, but I had to deal with all of that other shit first. Not only did no one have my back, but he cultivated this kind of behavior."

———————————

Talk about a toxic environment! You're left wondering: "Who is watching me? Who's going to run and give negative information to my boss?" These managers cultivate a sense of worry and paranoia that are utterly agonizing for the people on their team.

THE SPOTLIGHT SNATCHER

Some malignant managers will do whatever it takes to make themselves look good while keeping you down. They have no interest in giving you credit or recognizing the excellent work you do. They don't want to showcase what you've done so that others in the organization can see. At best, they never mention you; you're just the anonymous hard worker behind the curtain. At worst, they will claim your work as their own. For example, one client worked in a fast-paced environment where big projects had to be turned around on a dime. She worked long, exhausting hours on one project with the idea not only to deliver the expected results but also to please her boss. It worked at first: Her boss complimented her and thanked her, saying, "This is because of you."

"But then at the subsequent big celebration event, she didn't even mention me! Jealousy? I don't know. She would never give me credit for big things. When I got a key client back, she took credit for the achievement. It was so exhausting. There was nothing I could do to make her acknowledge my work and contribution."

This kind of behavior extends both to completed work and to ideas for making the organization better. These bosses will steal them all! And of course, there's a chilling effect on their direct reports' creativity, enthusiasm, and engagement. Why would you work hard and bring your best self when there's literally no benefit to you?

"I proposed ideas, and he was initially enthusiastic about me working on them, but then later said, 'Never mind, I'll take it from here.' He claimed and presented the ideas as his own after that. Turned out this was happening to others in the department, too. People stopped talking in meetings, not wanting him to claim their ideas and projects."

Spotlight Snatchers are also hesitant to give you access to important executives or customers, as they try to hoard the attention of decision makers and VIPs. They will often try to prevent you from presenting your work at, participating in, or even attending the higher-visibility meetings.

———————————

"I would set up meetings with marketing departments, and he would tell me, 'Do not speak, do not ask questions, pretend you're not here.' I was miserable because I had good relationships with clients. He was so controlling; he wanted to take credit for everything! Even when I could see they weren't understanding his ideas and pitches, I couldn't say anything. I felt so frustrated, stuck, and angry."

———————————

In many cases, these bosses think that giving you credit, visibility, or access to senior-level folks is a risk to their own status. They may feel threatened by you, believing that somehow your success will make them look less valuable. In some ways, their behavior may overlap the micromanager's—everything has to go through them, and they need to control the work, as if that proves their value to the company. If *you* own it, that might jeopardize their status! One client's boss acted like that:

———————————

"She felt threatened by me. I never wanted her job, but I made her nervous. She was always trying to cut me down. She would avoid giving me the information I needed. She was not invested in my growth or improvement. When I got an approval to do a speaking engagement, that bothered her. When I got looped into emails, she got irate! She would tell me to stop saying things in meetings,

saying, 'You take up too much space.' The only way I could please her was by keeping silent. She almost had this expression of joy when I said nothing in a meeting."

———————————

Knowing in our hearts that this behavior comes from their own deep insecurity helps explain the behavior, but it doesn't make it any less painful. You feel stuck in a situation where you can never move forward. You're stymied by the very person who should be helping you contribute at a high level and advance your career.

THE WORK-LIFE BALANCE BREAKER

My clients are all hardworking and career-oriented. Many of them are very accomplished managers and executives who readily take on extra assignments, pitch in to meet organizational needs and deadlines, and pursue opportunities for career growth. Most people I've coached and interviewed work long hours, often way beyond 40 hours per week. But malignant managers abuse this willingness to work hard. They give unreasonable assignments at all hours and completely disrespect their direct reports' personal lives. To them, there are few if any boundaries between work and personal time. They try to make work a round-the-clock obsession. Resistance and push-back are futile because the manager controls your job security. Take this experience:

———————————

"My boss would call at random hours just to see if our phones were on and how long it would take us to answer. He would phone at 9:00 a.m. on a Sunday, so even on the weekend when you thought

you might be able to relax, you couldn't. In all the years I worked for him, I can't remember a single time when he called because it was an actual emergency or even a legitimate urgent need. And domination of our lives carried into the workday. He once said, 'If you leave the building and your secretary doesn't know where you are, you will be fired.'"

———

There's a pretty big failure of empathy here, as these managers truly seem not to care whether you have a life outside of work. Sometimes they themselves work extremely long hours and take no time for their own personal lives. In these cases, their behavior makes a twisted kind of sense as you realize they're asking you to do what they also do. They have no regard for their own lives outside of work, so why would they have any regard for yours?

But some malignant managers have no problem asking you to sacrifice your life outside of work while they take care of themselves. One client's boss came in at 11:00 a.m. most days, and even took long lunches to manage personal business. Then he would stay until 8:00 or 9:00 p.m. and demand that my client stay too, saying, "It's your job." Here was another client's experience:

———

"She logged off at 6:00 p.m. because she had her own commitments, but she expected me to work into the evening. She would ask for deliverables on weekends after I had worked 12–16 hour days during the week. She actually said that people without children have no excuse not to keep working! At one point I told her, as nicely and gently as I could, that this pace was not sustainable. But as soon as I pushed back, she viewed me as the enemy."

———

Another variation on this theme is the manager who has no qualms not only sacrificing your personal time, but also taking credit for the work you've done. They're a combination of the Work-Life Balance Breaker and the Spotlight Snatcher. Here's how one client described his boss:

"He would make big promises to other execs on Friday afternoon for key deliverables by Monday afternoon. He would make these promises because he literally had no idea what it took to do the work and he didn't care. He asked me to do the project, of course, and he'd walk out the door on Friday at 4:00 p.m. Then on Monday, he'd take the work and present it as his own. He never invited his people to the table. He'd cozy up with the Executive VP one-on-one. We were left holding the bag."

Just to reiterate: Almost all of us have to (even want to!) work extra hours at times, whether there's a big project or presentation coming up, or an organizational emergency, or a staff shortage that requires others to fill the gap for a time. But under normal circumstances, we know that these long-hour days are temporary; there's a light at the end of the tunnel. With normal managers, there's also some appreciation for going above and beyond and taking on duties outside the typical scope of your role. You might even get some kind of recognition!

With malignant managers, these experiences of work overload are sustained and continuous. There's no end in sight at all. And there are no thanks or awards—certainly no apologies nor even some basic sympathy or appreciation that you might have a long commute after a long day. It feels endless and totally disrespectful. And sadly, the impacts of this kind of malignant behavior are predictable: stress, burnout, exhaustion, ill health, and tremendous resentment, not to mention the radiating impacts on your family members and personal life.

THE NEGLECTOR

As much as the other types of malignant behaviors are "in your face," sometimes the issue is the *absence* of management. With some bosses, their management boils down to nothing; they leave you on your own to figure things out. They never give you any feedback unless something has gone horribly wrong—the old "no news is good news" phenomenon. Everything is a priority, except talking with you. They don't engage with you and your team, and they don't seem to understand or care about the work you're doing. They are totally hands off, expecting you to figure out whatever needs to be done. You can expect no training, no mentorship, and no support.

For those who like autonomy and hate being micromanaged, this type of manager feels a bit like a blessing at first! But, over time, the effect of this kind of management takes a toll. You get no input on how you're doing, so you start to feel unsure if you're doing well at all. You get no support for your career development, so you don't know where you're going or how to get there. You feel aimless, unsteady on your feet, and you may feel set up for failure. Eventually you start to question everything about your performance and your career choice. It's especially painful if prior managers were there for you in all the right ways.

This kind of management looks like very infrequent meetings, which are usually canceled at the last minute anyway. There's never a performance review or a career discussion.

"I made appointments with her to discuss issues with my projects, ask questions, and gather input, but somehow she would always leave before. The message was: 'I don't have time for your stupid meeting.'"

Occasionally there is a meeting, but there's rarely (if ever) any helpful input or follow-up. It's like they're going through the motions to meet with you out of obligation, but they're not invested in helping you with your work or career. They're perfectly content with the status quo. From their perspective, a discussion might lead to some kind of change, and they have no interest in change. It seems they'd prefer that you just stay quiet and satisfied with the way things are. Or worse, they're just not thinking about you at all. Your goals or ambitions don't seem to factor in.

"He knew that I had pretty much mastered my responsibilities and was eager to grow career-wise. I asked him a couple of times if I could contribute on an additional project to learn new skills, and he just said, 'I'll think about it,' but never got back to me."

Because they're so disengaged, the neglectful manager doesn't go to bat for you and your team, either. If you need resources, you're out of luck. If you need protection from unreasonable expectations or problems that are outside your control, they won't have your back. They may do a good job of pretending to upper management that they're engaged, but in reality, they're not at all.

"Our boss would be in meetings and say nothing. My peers and I would be under fire, but he would let us flounder. Not only did he never stand up for us, he never even cut a meeting short to say, 'We'll get back to you.' He literally had no idea what we were up to, so he just let us take the blame for anything that went wrong, as if we weren't his team!"

While this type of malignancy is a bit more under the radar than some of the others, those who experience it are left super confused, frustrated, and upset. It's not long before you might veer into self-blame, lower self-confidence, and surely loss of goodwill toward the organization.

Over the years, my clients have shared their horrible—even traumatic—experiences, and these seven types of malignant managers have emerged. But as mentioned earlier, *your* boss may show behaviors from more than one type. This is unfortunately pretty common too. Like the one who's verbally abusive and also demands that you are available at all hours of the day and night. Or the one who will complain to you about others behind their backs one day, and then scream at you the next. Or the one who will micromanage every project, and also completely ignore your requests for feedback. Not every manager fits neatly into one description; sometimes they bring a basketful of malignant behaviors to the office.

There are also a few traits that can cut across these types. For one, malignant managers can be quite charming to those above them. They are masters at playing the game, hiding abusive and harsh behaviors from those who might disapprove. They pretend that all is well and they say all the right things. If you get to witness this kiss-up kind of behavior, it's sickening, since you know how it *really* is on a day-to-day level. It's also extremely frustrating because you have no idea how to get the truth out there.

Lack of empathy is also quite common among malignant managers. It makes sense . . . . If they could put themselves in their people's shoes and emotionally understand how they feel and what they're going through, it would be unnatural to treat them harshly, humiliate or neglect them, demand that they work insane hours, and so on. Somehow, it seems that many of these managers have a gap in this core area of emotional intelligence. Or, they purposefully close off their empathetic tendencies so as not to seem weak or soft in the eyes of their team members or their own bosses.

Another common characteristic across malignant types is the tendency to play favorites. Some treat everybody horribly, but many choose to have allies for a while. They decide—based on some mysterious criteria—that some member or members of the team are their favorites, treating them well and offering support and opportunities. If you're not with the "in" crowd, you may decide that the treatment you're getting must be because of something you're doing wrong. You worry and blame yourself, but if you stick around long enough, you'll likely see that there's a rotating membership in the favorites' club. These managers can't let anyone get too close or powerful, so they find a way to knock some of these folks off the list. If you become a favorite, you know you can't really trust your status. There's no safe spot with malignant managers.

One last undercurrent across some hideous managers is sexism. I've only seen the pattern in male managers—like the Humiliator who told one client to lose 30 pounds. He never would have said such a vicious thing to a male colleague. Or like this story I heard from another client:

―――――――――――

"He warned us not to be late to staff meetings, as he would start on time and we would miss important info. He yelled at me a couple of times when a prior meeting ran over and I couldn't get to his meeting on time. But when his favorite person was late to the meeting—a man, by the way, in a department full of women— he'd say, 'Let's wait another few minutes for [so-and-so] to arrive.'"

―――――――――――

Or another client, who got a new boss based in Europe.

―――――――――――

"At first, he was just plain rude to the women in his group. Then, he was hiring for a position and there were four internal candidates—three women and one man. When the man announced he was leaving the company and taking himself out of the running, the boss said, 'Oh no, you can't leave—I'm going to give you the role and elevate you.' This was before there were any interviews! The women were so angry. They reported this and many other issues to HR, but nothing was done. It was clear that the culture had changed, and this guy was only going to take care of other men in the group. Over nine months, five women quit. I kept thinking, 'What's wrong with me that I'm still here?'"

―――――――――――

If you care about fairness, collaboration, and career growth, work can get pretty bleak when you have a malignant manager. The system will protect them, often for many years. They chew through good people and spit them out. You can find ways to cope and manage for a time, but you may not be able to outlast a malignant manager. It may look like they'll be protected forever. I will note, though, that they often get their "just desserts" later—eventually the complaints get too loud, or the team's performance suffers too much, or their behavior starts to affect the bottom line and they get forced out. When you find out they're gone, you'll feel vindicated! But if you're suffering right now, you can't get your hopes up for that. You just have to find your way through it—you need strategies for survival—and that's what the next section is all about.

KEY TAKEAWAYS

1. If you're not sure whether you have a malignant manager, answer the five questions at the beginning of this chapter. Answering "yes" to all or most of them is a good indicator that your manager is indeed malignant.
2. This book identifies seven types of malignant managers. I call them the Humiliator, the Hyper-Controller, the Conniver, the Rollercoaster, the Spotlight Snatcher, the Work-Life Balance Breaker, and the Neglector. Your boss may fit into one or more of these types.
3. There are a few traits that cut across all the types, including a strong ability to "manage up," a lack of empathy, and a tendency to play favorites.
4. You may want to figure out *why* your manager behaves the way they do, but knowing the reason does not justify their behavior.

Strategies for Coping with a Malignant Manager— When You're Not Ready to Quit

The biggest challenge in dealing with a malignant manager is trying to figure out how to get some relief. That relief usually comes in two forms: (1) finding ways to survive, make your experience in your current job better, and by extension, diminish the negative impact of your manager, and (2) finding a way out of your current job and into a new one.

In this chapter, I'll present multiple strategies for coping while you're still working with and for your current manager, because I know and have seen that **quitting is often neither desirable nor possible**. Perhaps this is a great job that you worked really hard to get.

It may pay well and have benefits that your family depends on. Maybe you're the only breadwinner in the family. Or maybe the commute is ideal and other opportunities would likely be farther away. Or maybe you've only just started this job, and you don't want to "job hop." There may not be another job like this one, or it may feel that way. Understandably, you might feel intense pressure to stick it out, at least for a while.

The other challenge with quitting is that it can be scary and potentially detrimental to do so before you have another job lined up. It's very hard to predict how long it could take to find another job, and during that period, you won't be paid. The longer the search goes on, the more anxious you might become about your financial situation. That anxiety or even desperation could lead you to take another job that's not really good for you, just to have a paycheck coming in.

Quitting can also wreak havoc on the job search process itself. You may have heard that it's easier to find a job when you're employed, and this is true. Quitting creates a gap in your career history, and prospective employers often prefer candidates without recent gaps. Some recruiters search on LinkedIn only for candidates who are currently employed. Even when you land interviews, you can expect questions about why you left your job. You'll have to explain the reasons for your decision without disparaging your past employer because negative talk nearly always backfires.

For all of these reasons, I tend to encourage most of my clients to hang on as long as possible, even if they're in a truly horrible work environment, so that their path to a new role will be smoother and less stressful. There are exceptions to this guidance, of course, like if the manager's treatment is taking a horrific toll on your health. Remember my client who lost 30 pounds due to the stress he felt? He needed to get out of there ASAP. But short of these kinds of extremes, there are benefits to staying and coping before you make your move out of the organization.

So what are those strategies for making your current job more tolerable, lessening the toll it takes on you, and gaining back a sense of power and agency? In the following pages, I will highlight a variety of steps you can take on and off the job—including general strategies no matter what type of malignant manager you have—as well as specific strategies for your particular type of manager.

Then, in the next chapter, I will highlight strategies you can take to plan for and (eventually) make an exit, whenever the time is right. These strategies have all worked well for my clients at one time or another. May they be a resource for you as well.

DON'T SUFFER ALONE—TALK TO OTHERS & FIND ALLIES

If you're dealing with a malignant manager day in and day out, hopefully you're venting some of your frustrations and experiences to friends and family at home. Expressing what's happening is so valuable because it provides the opportunity to process recent events and let go of some of your most self-critical and painful thoughts and feelings. Bottling these up rarely works out well, as the horrible feelings tend to accumulate and fester. Sometimes, the pain becomes so intense that it shows up in the form of illness, sleeplessness, anger, and tears of frustration.

So go ahead and share with the folks who are part of your circle of support. They know you and love you and can help bolster your self-esteem and strength, which have probably been battered on the job. These people in your inner circle also have a long-term view. They remember how things were before you started working for your malignant manager. They can provide critical perspective, reminding you of the way things were in prior jobs and highlighting the truth about who you are as a person and as an employee.

"I spoke often with my friends—they helped me stay sane. These conversations set me back to normal faster."

Of course, there may be times when you feel that you would rather not burden people close to you with recurring complaints. Chances are, they're happy to support you, no matter what. But if it starts to seem like you are overloading your inner circle too much, consider turning to a therapist or coach for additional support and perspective. More on this below in the *Take Care of Yourself* section.

I also urge you to find allies at work—people you can safely confide in and who will relate to what's happening to you. The tendency among many of my clients has been to keep their concerns to themselves, at least initially. It may take a while to know who to trust, and even then, it's hard to know how to broach the subject. Maybe it feels unprofessional to complain. Or if you're new on the job, perhaps you're still wondering if you are the one to blame for your manager's behavior.

But, if your manager has more than one direct report, it's likely that there are others around you who are quietly struggling with the same fears and feelings about the work environment in general and your manager in particular. Listen carefully for hints people may drop about ways they feel mistreated. If there's a social gathering outside of work when the boss isn't there, you may hear some murmurs or outright complaints. These are the moments when you may realize that it's ok to talk with your coworkers about the issues with your boss.

When you have someone else you can share your experience and feelings with, it validates what you're going through and helps you feel less alone. Other folks can also provide invaluable perspective, helping you see more clearly that the behavior you're dealing with is not your fault. Here's what two clients had to say:

———————————————

"It was hard to admit to peers that I was suffering. I took too long to ask. I kept it to myself for a long time. But then I started a conversation with others who worked for her several years earlier. It was helpful to hear about their terrible experiences. It helped to see that it was a pattern."

"Understanding that he did that to so many other people made me feel less singled out. It was almost like having a support group of people he'd hurt or destroyed. Leaning on them, reaching out, and being supportive of others was incredibly helpful."

———————————————

Sharing with others is also empowering. You realize that you are allies in the fight against injustice. You are a buddy network, offering each other an outlet for your pain as well as ideas for how to contend with the situation.

———————————————

"All of us direct reports would complain to each other. We created a chat channel where we would just vent about her. It helped us figure out ways to manage around her."

———————————————

There may also be others in the organization, outside of your work group, who see what's going on and can provide moral support and validation. You might not feel comfortable reaching out to them, but they may contact you or otherwise signal that they see what is happening and they support you. Knowing that you have these kinds of allies can bolster your sense of worth and encourage you when your strength is flagging.

––––––––––––

"I feel lucky because my boss's peers are supportive of me. They tell me things like, 'We know what great work you're doing.' They don't understand why my boss is treating me this way. They see what he's doing to me. They often ask me: 'How do you deal with it?' Their support didn't fundamentally change the situation, but I didn't feel so alone."

––––––––––––

To be seen, heard, and supported is critical when you're suffering under any malignant manager, no matter which type you have. Building a support network—both outside of work and on the job—can help sustain you through the difficult times and counteract those negative impacts on your self-esteem, performance, and health, like those discussed in Chapter I.

RECONNECT WITH WHAT
YOU HAVE ACHIEVED

Regardless of the type of malignant manager you have, your ongoing experience can take a toll on self-esteem, leaving you with thoughts like: "I must be doing something wrong," or, "Maybe I'm not cut out for this work." These kinds of thoughts are not only crushing in the moment, but they may interfere with your ability to perform, as well as your eventual success in applying and selling yourself for a new job.

One way to counteract these thoughts is to start capturing successes you've had in your career—to remember and reconnect with who you are and what you do well. You may really have to force yourself to do this if your self-esteem has plummeted or if you're feeling beaten down every day. Looking at prior performance reviews (if you have them) is one way to jog your memory about past projects and past impacts you've had on the job. Asking friends and former colleagues may also help if you really can't recall what makes you good at what you do.

"I talked to friends to decompress and remind me what I was good at. One of them asked me, 'When was a time you were at peak performance?' This generated a very specific visualization and helped me remember a time when I knew my abilities."

Another specific tool for remembering and capturing your achievements and skills is the "CAR" story. The acronym CAR stands for "Challenge, Action, Results." You start by writing down a challenge you have faced at work (beyond your challenges with your boss!). It could be the launch of a new product, a major project with a tight deadline, a sudden change with a customer, a financial shift that required you to cut costs . . . . Any challenge will work. Think back on the last year or so and recall a challenge you had to contend with. Or, if the last year was all negative, then go further back. In most jobs, there are many expected and unexpected challenges, so you should be able to think of at least one. Briefly write down the scope of the **Challenge**—what was the problem you faced?

Once you have identified the Challenge, write down the **Actions** you took to address it. There are probably many things you did, and that's completely fine. Jot them all down.

Then, most importantly, capture the **Results** of your actions. What came of your effort? Identify results that have metrics if possible, like costs saved or revenues grown or a deadline met or scores improved. But the results don't have to be quantifiable. There can be a variety of outcomes, like a problem averted, positive feedback received, a new process or system implemented, an award earned, or a relationship strengthened.

When you write a CAR story, it gives you an opportunity to reconnect with something you have done well at work and to remember outcomes that really mattered to the organization or your team. If you set yourself the goal to write four or five CAR stories, you'll start to paint a picture of your own effectiveness. I often hear clients say things like, "Yeah, that really turned out well," or, "I forgot about how important that experience was to the team," or even, "I really made a difference."

"The CAR story structure helped me to identify some significant accomplishments during my tenure here. It pushed me to really sit and think about those things that I am proud of, that were successful and meaningful. The format was concise and allowed for an encapsulated moment. Especially because this environment feels

like it's sucking my energy and life away right now. It felt good to remember and write down some things I've achieved."

Writing CAR stories can be a simple but powerful way to remind yourself of all the assets you bring to work and all that you have delivered. No matter your type of manager nor how much your self-esteem has suffered, the process of capturing these stories can help you rewind to the times in your job or career when you knew you were performing well and bring those experiences right up to the surface. In addition to helping you feel stronger, there's a side bonus to writing the stories: They're a gold mine for resume content and interview responses! More on those later.

TAKE CARE OF YOURSELF (REALLY DO IT)

What are the things you do to take care of yourself? Go running? Do yoga? Walk in nature? Meditate? Listen to music? Get extra sleep? Spend time with friends and family? Talk with a therapist? ***Whatever your go-to solution or solutions, make time for them now.*** If you don't have a solid tool or set of tools you use, this may be the moment to identify something you can do regularly to give yourself a physical and/or emotional boost.

Your malignant manager is already draining your energy and self-esteem. Your physical health may even be suffering. You need to refill your bucket. A common side effect of reporting to a bad manager is that you feel exhausted and miserable at the end of the day, and all you want to do with your downtime is watch TV, play video games, or scroll on social media to take your mind off things.

Unfortunately, sitting still and looking at screens has a way of sapping your energy even more. That's when scheduling time to take care of yourself—*even a few moments each day*—is all the more critical. Here's what two of my clients had to say:

"Exercise was key—I went running a lot, even if I had to do it in the wee hours of the morning. Getting away from it all with physical activity was something I could do for myself."

"I got into cooking. It was a way to spend time with my family, making healthy meals and doing something totally positive and creative."

In a way, taking care of yourself can be the positive flipside to the horrible health impacts discussed in Chapter I. Your difficult work situation can be an impetus to prioritize yourself and your physical and mental health. Research continues to show that physical exercise has a positive effect on mental wellness, including reducing depression, anxiety, and stress, and improving sleep.[6,7] Making time for exercise and self-care will have cumulative and lasting benefits that will help you reset your nervous system and build back your physical and mental strength so you can deal more effectively with your malignant manager.

---

[6]Christopher James Holland, et al., "Exercise and mental health: a vital connection," *British Journal of Sports Medicine* 58, no. 13 (2024), https://bjsm.bmj.com/content/58/13/691.

[7]Majd A. Alnawwar, et al., "The Effect of Physical Activity on Sleep Quality and Sleep Disorder: A Systematic Review," *Cureus* 15, no. 8 (2023), https://doi.org/10.7759/cureus.43595.

For some, therapy is a key tool for managing stress and rebuilding self-confidence, as a good therapist can help you understand and manage your emotions and develop solutions for navigating a difficult situation. If you have access to a therapist, you can use a session (or more than one) to share all the horrible things that are happening at work, which can be helpful if you want to spend less time venting to your family and friends.

"I'm a strong believer in therapy. She helped me not go down the path of wondering what's wrong with me. She helped me get through some anxiety and fear and not get too out of control with what wasn't true. Not burdening my spouse was also helpful. Working with her gave me ideas to help my own direct reports as well."

A therapist might also be able to help you with strategies to control your sensitivity to your manager's behavior and avoid making the problem worse. For example, if you're super sensitive to criticism, your manager's critiques might lead you to shrink smaller and do less well at work, thus leading to more criticism and setting up a vicious cycle. The therapeutic process could help you keep your reactions in check and break recurring patterns that exacerbate the situation. Navigating your own emotions in a more productive way will at a minimum help you feel better and stronger at work. There's a chance you might also have a positive influence on your manager's behavior.

If you don't have a therapist, your employer may have a free Employee Assistance Program (EAP) that can connect you with confidential therapeutic support. *Psychology Today* also offers referral resources for therapists in every geographic region of the US, including those who will accept your health insurance.

Whether you do therapy or not, there may be other relevant resources you can tap, such as health, wellness, and mindset podcasts that offer information, ideas, and stories. One client shared that podcasts like these offered very helpful perspectives on how others have overcome hardship, reinforcing the feeling that she wasn't alone, and helping her sustain her sense of balance.

Another self-care strategy that some of my clients have used is practicing some kind of ritual right before work to build up a sense of strength and confidence going into each day. A few examples include:

"I played the song 'Brave' by Sara Bareilles over and over again in my ears on the way to work. That was a real anthem for me."

"I meditated and breathed every day before I got out of the car."

"I visualized a protective bubble around me, one that repelled the negative words and energy. I could even wash off the outside of it in my mind! It helped me maintain a sense of a boundary and distance from the situation."

"I got to work so much earlier than others to get things done while I had a clear head. It was a way for me to be on offense for an hour and a half before I had to be on defense for the rest of the day."

I recognize that it's much easier to talk about doing good things for yourself than to actually do them. If we're exhausted and beaten down, it's extremely challenging to channel time and energy into exercising, meditating, or finding a therapist. If our brain and nervous system are in reactive fight-or-flight mode, we're not poised to take proactive, steady, longer-term strategies. If you're being cut down at work, it may be extra hard to build yourself back up or even feel like you deserve to give yourself something good. The barriers to self-care start to feel very big. We can even get stuck in another kind of vicious cycle—feeling bad about ourselves at work, feeling low-energy outside of work, not taking care of ourselves, feeling bad about not taking care of ourselves, not bringing our strongest selves to work, not doing well at work, feeling bad about ourselves at work . . . and repeat.

If you're having trouble getting started or finding time to incorporate anything that feels like taking care of yourself, please don't beat yourself up over that and compound the problem. Set small goals, like taking five deep breaths between meetings, making sure you have water at your side, or giving yourself a couple minutes to stand up and move around every hour. Give yourself a hand by setting timers, scheduling some self-care time into your calendar, or asking a friend to keep you accountable. And don't commit initially to doing something every day or every week. Start with *once* and then see how you feel. Set an intention for the day: "What's one thing I can do to show myself a little love today?"

It doesn't really matter what you choose to do, or how much time you dedicate, as long as you intentionally do *something* to take care of *you*. Work already takes up a lot of time and headspace. If you're dealing with a malignant manager, it consumes even more of your attention as you seek ways to navigate a difficult, stressful, or even damaging situation. On top of work, your family and personal commitments may also demand a lot of time and energy. Even small amounts of self-care are a way of tipping the balance back in your favor, at least a little bit.

TAKE TIME OFF

Time away from the office and work environment can give you the space to put work into perspective—to realize that your job doesn't define your value as a person. Some of us can get to a place where we feel work is our life. While our jobs are important, of course, they don't have to—and really shouldn't—take over. Time away can help you reclaim a sense of self, remember who you are outside of work, and put problems with your malignant manager in their proper place.

When you're in the thick of a demanding and stressful situation, it can be very difficult to do any of this. If it feels daunting to take time away from a high-pressure job, start small—by scheduling a three-day weekend, perhaps, or leaving early on a Friday—and aim to truly unplug from work emails and other communications during that time off. This approach can really be helpful if your manager is a Work-Life Balance Breaker, and may also provide a respite from a Humiliator, Hyper-Controller, or Conniver.

"We were always under the gun and scrambling at work, and I always felt so much pressure from my boss to get everything done. But I also desperately needed relief. So I started blocking dates in advance—sometimes just a day or two—and these little bits of time off were like an oasis for me. They gave me a chance to rest and recharge or do things just for me."

A real vacation may also give you vital distance and perspective to recalibrate the importance of work in your life. Especially in the United States, studies show that we tend not to take advantage of the vacation time available to us.[8] Doing so can be part of your arsenal of strategies in dealing with your manager.

Now, if your health is suffering greatly—if, for example, you're experiencing frequent headaches, difficulty sleeping, debilitating anxiety, inability to eat, or other significant health issues—you may want to consider requesting a medical leave of absence. Consult your organization's policies on what documentation you'll need and what process to follow to request one.

A leave could provide the opportunity to regroup and heal with rest, dietary changes, doctors' visits, medication . . . whatever you need to get well. Maybe you can start to implement some self-care habits, like those discussed in the last section, and you'll have the time to establish a routine that could potentially continue even when you return to work. Perhaps this healing period can help you reconnect with your innate strengths and self-confidence.

Importantly, a leave of absence can also give you the space and perspective you need to figure out your next steps. You can assess whether you are strong and healthy enough to return to your job. You can perhaps identify some strategies or steps you can take to be less affected by your malignant manager and the difficult work environment, knowing that the situation will likely not be much different if you return. You can also make a more clearheaded determination about whether you want or feel you need to quit. One very

---

[8] Shradha Dinesh and Kim Parker, "More than 4 in 10 U.S. workers don't take all their paid time off," Pew Research Center, August 10, 2023, https://www.pewresearch.org/short-reads/2023/08/10/more-than-4-in-10-u-s-workers-dont-take-all-their-paid-time-off/.

senior-level client formulated a plan for what specifically to ask for when she went back to the office:

"I was so stressed and couldn't sleep, and then I had a cancer scare. So I went on sick leave and really focused on dealing with my health issues. While I was out and getting better, I decided that I would return in time for a major event with the CEO and then ask for a new role. If she wouldn't help with that, then I was going to make a six-month plan for my exit. It became clear that I needed a change. And I did end up leaving."

Sometimes you need distance from the situation in order to think about it clearly. When you feel stuck, you may also feel desperate, like, "I just want to escape!" If you're on leave, you have time to process your options and assess whether leaving is really the right choice. As another client put it simply:

"Now that I'm on short-term disability because of the stress, my brain is unscrambling a bit and I now know I have to leave."

If you decide that you do want to resign, you can also start preparing for your departure while you're out. The primary purpose of a medical leave is to get healthier, of course, so I don't necessarily advise filling up the time with job search activities, which bring their own kind of stress. But even mental preparation to quit takes some time, so the leave period can give you the chance to come to grips with the fact that you need to move on. You can also start dipping your toe into the search, perhaps through outreach and networking calls, or some work on your resume and LinkedIn profile. More on these strategies in a few pages.

SET BOUNDARIES

Depending on your type of manager, you may find it crucial to find ways to establish boundaries that protect you from malignant behavior. These boundaries can take a variety of forms. For example, if your manager is a Humiliator or Conniver, your best boundary might be distance. Avoiding interaction with this person as much as possible will limit the chance that you'll have a negative interaction and protect more of your work time.

"I avoided her as much as possible and tried to do my best work. I could walk a long way around to get to my office without passing hers. Years later, I can still picture that route I took, just so I wouldn't have to talk with her and be on the receiving end of her verbal attacks."

"I just didn't want to get caught up in the petty drama of talking about other people behind their backs. I always had a ready excuse—saying there was some meeting coming up, or a call I had to make, or a thing I had to take care of—just so I could avoid engaging in that nasty nonsense."

For those of you laboring under a Work-Life Balance Breaker, your boundary might have to be regular, clear communication (verbal and written) about your commitments outside of work. If you establish that there are firm lines between work and life that can't be crossed, it will be easier to stand your ground. There may be times when it's ok with you to stay late or work weekends, and maybe those become part of the compromise you make to retain the firmer boundaries.

"I told her that I had to leave on time every other Friday. She tried to make me feel guilty about it, but I was working late all the other days! Mostly, I felt I had to suck it up and pay my dues, but eventually protecting those Friday nights at least allowed me to go out of town to visit my partner on the weekends."

One way to establish a boundary with Hyper-Controller managers is to develop and send them a brief weekly status report or summary. This little report—in the same structure every week—should capture your progress on key projects or responsibilities during the week, your plans for next week, and brief notes on issues that need the manager's attention, if any. For a Hyper-Controller, this type of communication sets a boundary in a way—preventing them from demanding information, usually with no warning, about what you're doing or where some project stands. You keep them at bay by proactively giving them the information and control they crave, at a level of frequency that should satisfy their need to know.

"She doesn't always read my weekly summaries, but when she does, they do seem to calm her down a bit and satisfy her need to have a sense of control over everything that's going on."

If you have a Rollercoaster manager, your brief written reports can focus on summarizing agreements made during meetings, including what was asked for and what you will do. These notes—which can be quick emails, but should always be in a consistent format—offer a written record of proof that you can refer to if your Rollercoaster says, "I didn't ask for that!" or, "That's not what we agreed on!" If done consistently, they should help insulate you a bit from erratic changes of mind or impulsive requests. This approach isn't fail-safe, of course, and it won't keep your manager's emotions in control, but it could help avert at least a few unnecessary disagreements and stress.

A type of boundary you might be able to establish with a Neglector or Spotlight Snatcher is to find opportunities outside of your immediate work group to contribute on special projects. This might not always be possible, depending on the size of your organization and the intensity of your workload. But if you can seek your own extra projects elsewhere in the organization—ideally with someone who really values you—you might be able to elevate your contributions to the organization, strengthen your reputation, and accrue some additional achievements about which you can be really proud.

SEE THE LEARNING OPPORTUNITY

When you're in the thick of something dark and awful, it's hard to see a bright side. But I was pleasantly surprised that some of my clients consciously chose to take an important lesson from their horrible experiences with their malignant managers. For example, these clients focused on learning what NOT to do with their own teams. One client, who was not yet a manager, told me that he took mental notes every day on his manager's behaviors, gathering insights on what not to do and getting clear on how he would be different when he became a manager someday. He almost started to view the situation in a clinical and objective way, like a researcher taking notes about his observations. This helped him feel less mired in his current situation and more empowered.

Another client made a point of being the leader he wanted his own manager to be.

"That time I spent with my own team gave me a lot of peace of mind. It was work I could hang my hat on. I knew I was doing the right thing and giving them the support, resources, and guidance she never provided. I could see that they really benefited from the way I was managing them, too."

If you're a manager yourself, another related thing you can do is to make a point of shielding your own team from your manager. Preventing them from having to experience humiliation, erratic behavior, or unreasonable assignments may mean that you are in the proverbial line of fire, but you can then translate your boss's demands, accusations, or out-of-control behavior into more productive messages and collaborative strategies. You may also be able to advocate for your team members at times, representing their needs, showcasing their performance, asking for what they need, and overall, elevating your own skills as a team leader.

Whether you're a manager or not, you can also practice being an empathetic leader and a creator of positive culture. (A small handful of resources for improving your empathy and management skills are included in the Appendix to this book.) Cultivating these qualities will likely give you an emotional lift while also building skills that will be useful and valuable throughout your career—even if they're not valued in your current workplace. One client described it this way:

"I tried to reach out to people and be kind to them as a counter-point to all the negative feedback. I could see that people were thirsty for it. Even when I was feeling bad, it helped to reach out to others and give positive feedback. I saw the culture we could be, and I wanted to build it."

One last unexpected lesson you might be able to take from your situation is to cultivate empathy for your malignant manager. Believe me, I understand that this might not *ever* be possible—especially if your manager is particularly cruel, like the Humiliators, Connivers, and even Work-Life Balance Breakers can be. When you're beaten down, it's hard to think about having empathy for the person doing it to you.

But for some people, it's helpful to consider the circumstances that have made their managers behave the way they do. Maybe they are under tremendous pressure from the executives above them. Maybe they have little in the way of family and friends outside of work. Maybe they have an illness or pain they are dealing with . . . . Putting yourself in their shoes might help you see them differently and take the way they treat you less personally. Tapping your innate empathy skills might feel good and give you a sense of power as you manage your challenging relationship with your manager. Again, this may not be possible for you, and if so, that's ok—but I offer it here as a possible learning opportunity.

70   Breaking Free from a Malignant Manager

SHOULD YOU TALK TO HR?

If you're dealing with a malignant manager, there may come a point where you just feel that you need to report the manager's behavior to someone else, hoping that the organization itself might come to your aid. Because of its responsibility for employee matters, it makes logical sense to bring complaints to someone in the human resources department, if there is an established HR team in your organization. More on assessing your HR team below.

Many people who work in HR are good at their jobs and have chosen that career path because they care about people, are good listeners, and believe in justice and fair play. Of course, that doesn't describe everyone, but many fit that description.

Making the decision to go to HR, though, can be risky, so you really have to think it through and ask yourself some key questions— at least the ones that I share in the coming pages. You don't want to contact your HR representative if you fear that doing so could make your situation worse, as it did for this person:

"He found out I had gone to HR, and he got furious. He yelled at me for a few days, and then he shifted and started giving me the silent treatment, just leaving work on my desk."

Even though retaliation is illegal at the federal level, there are situations where the manager might take advantage of the imbalance in power and retaliate anyway.[9] Retaliation can be

---

[9]"Retaliation," Equal Employment Opportunity Commission, accessed June 5, 2025, https://www.eeoc.gov/retaliation.

subtle, like giving you the cold shoulder, giving interesting projects to someone else, or talking behind your back in ways that harm your reputation.

On the other hand, going to HR could be a good course of action in certain circumstances, especially if it helps the HR team assemble a record of a pattern of behavior on your manager's part. **But it's important to understand that there are very few quick solutions that even the best HR team can implement.** If you go to HR, it may seem like you finally summoned up your courage to make a complaint and nothing came of it. A number of my clients have voiced this frustration: "I went to HR and they did nothing."

The reality is that sometimes you're right—they've done nothing other than make note of your complaint. But sometimes they actually *do* take action, and you just don't see it. They may ask other people in the department if they have seen some of the same issues you have. Like this client who heard from other members of her team:

"They're questioning all of us about how he's treating you, and we're telling them everything."

Your HR representative may end up talking with your manager, providing some suggestions and coaching, and trying to secure promises of better behavior. They may put a plan in place to get your manager a coach. They might contact your manager's manager to discuss and explore what's happening in your department. Even if HR takes some of these actions, though, there probably won't be any immediate relief.

"I was a temp, and after six weeks of my boss screaming at me and humiliating me, I went to HR and said, 'I'm not the person for him.' HR said, 'We're going to address this,' but it went on for seven more months!"

So, while it might be possible for HR to help you, there are a few questions that you should ask yourself before going to them. These questions include:

Does your organization have an established HR team with someone who is clearly responsible for handling employee relations matters? Depending on your organization's size or structure, there may only be one, or a small number of, HR staff, and they may only focus on things like benefits administration, hiring, payroll, and workplace policies. On a small team like this, you may not have an HR person who is trained to navigate manager-employee issues or disputes, investigate concerns, provide coaching to managers or staff, or recommend solutions. It would be fruitless to bring your concerns to an HR staff member in this kind of situation.

"In my local office, the word among all of us was, 'Don't go to HR,' if you want anything beyond the basics. I might have tried to reach out to someone at the global level, but it just felt too daunting and unlikely to work."

Larger companies and organizations, however, should have an HR person assigned to your unit or team, and that person would likely have the experience and training to work with you. They still may fail to act, but in general, it's in their best interest to try to resolve performance issues and mitigate any risks to the organization.

Is your manager's behavior illegal or a clear violation of company policy? Sexual harassment, racism, use of drugs or alcohol during work . . . . These are all complaints that really must be addressed by the human resources team. If you can document the violation(s) and identify those who can corroborate the behavior, all the better. But as discussed throughout this book, many malignant behaviors don't necessarily rise to this level of severity. As one client said: "HR knew she went up to the line but didn't cross it."

Is your manager's malignant behavior part of a pattern that has persisted for some time? Have you documented specific examples of the behavior? Are there any others on your team who have witnessed the behavior, including the specific examples you have collected? Are there any other indicators, like survey data, that point to a problem with your manager? One of the challenges with going to HR is that they have to evaluate your perception of your manager versus the manager's perception of their own behavior, as well as the manager's perception of *you*. Your manager may believe that their own behavior is fine and may claim that you are simply complaining because you have received tough feedback. If you're in a he-said-she-said kind of situation—your perception versus theirs—it will be very hard for HR to take any kind of helpful action. They may chalk it up to bad chemistry, a bad day, or worse, they might agree with the manager's assessment that you're the problem. Unfortunately, this client ended up in a situation like this:

"I debated if I should, but I ended up complaining to HR. I just felt, 'I'm not going to continue like this.' It was enough already. They asked if I wanted to write this up, and then they did an investigation,

but they said they couldn't find corroboration, so they decided they
would terminate me. They offered me a severance package with a
promise not to disclose what had gone on. It didn't work out the way
I had hoped at all, but at least I added to the case against her."

If others have made similar complaints about the manager, however, that may carry valuable weight in HR's evaluation of the situation. If employee survey results are poor in your manager's unit
and validate some of your complaints, all the better. If there has
been high employee turnover on your team, HR will also take note
of that. The more data you can marshal to reinforce your claims,
the greater your chances of triggering an investigation and getting
support from HR.

Do you trust your HR person? If you are afraid of your manager, concerned about retaliation, and nervous about doing anything
to jeopardize your job, the only way you can consider going to HR
is if you're sure that doing so won't backfire. You have to assess how
well you know the HR contact, how they have handled sensitive
information in the past, and how close they are to your manager.
One way to test the waters with HR is to start with a discussion of
a smaller issue. If the response is helpful, perhaps that will give you
confidence that you might get some help with a bigger issue.

Ultimately, you need to ask yourself: If I ask the HR person to
keep a conversation confidential, how likely would they be to do so?
Understand that they are required to break confidence if you share
illegal behavior on your manager's part, but in other cases, you should
only go to HR if you feel there's trust between you. Unfortunately,
there are many out there who just don't reach this level of trust in
their HR team, like this client:

"I didn't trust HR, because they were close to my boss. My boss, her boss, and the HR person all hung out together and talked shit about everybody on the team."

How "protected" is your manager? As discussed in an earlier chapter, some managers are great about "managing up" and have very strong allies at senior levels. Even when there is data to verify their egregious behavior, the political environment in the organization (the manager's manager and other powers that be) might protect the manager. In order to take any action, the HR person would need the higher-ups to buy in, and they just might not agree. In these situations, you can't expect that going to HR will help your cause, at least not in the short term.

What do you really want HR to do? Above all, if you decide to go to HR, you want to be clear and realistic about what you hope to achieve. They may be there for you, and they probably want to do right by you and the organization, but they also have a responsibility to represent the manager. They won't be able to fire your manager, at least not right away (unless it's an egregious violation); they don't want to get sued for wrongful termination, and it will take time for them to marshal a case.

At a minimum, they might be able to give you some support in navigating the situation. They also might be able to facilitate a conversation between you and your manager, provide your manager with some coaching, or even help you move into a new area. But again, none of these solutions will be quick. The clearer and more realistic you can be about what you hope to get out of your conversation with HR, the less likely you will be to emerge disappointed.

SHOULD YOU TALK TO YOUR BOSS'S BOSS?

At some point, it may cross your mind that you'd like to report the problems you're having with your manager to *their* boss. You may think something like: "If they only knew what their direct report was doing to their staff, they'd do something about it." And that might be true, but it also might not.

Generally, it's an ill-advised strategy. Neither your manager nor their manager is likely to appreciate that you "went over your boss's head" to try to settle your issues. The expectation in most professional environments is that you should resolve problems directly and not escalate them.

You also may not be privy to your boss's relationship with their manager. Your boss may have been doing a great job of "managing up" over the years, and they may be viewed very favorably. Their boss may have even played a role in getting them promoted to their current role and have a personal interest in seeing them succeed.

There may be circumstances in which talking to your boss's boss is ok, but it has to make sense for your situation. For example, I have had a handful of clients who worked directly with or for the boss's boss in the past. They had a strong, established, and friendly relationship, and it was clearly safe to go to them for guidance and input.

———————

"I had worked for her before, and we were very close, so I felt really comfortable going to her with my issues. I still tried to provide specific examples of the problem and tried to be unemotional, though. I wanted her to hear me and take the situation seriously. I think she did end up talking to my boss and things got marginally better."

———————

In some cases, the boss's boss may approach you directly and ask for input about your manager. Perhaps some complaints have filtered up, and this conversation would present an opportunity to share some insights, especially if you have another colleague or two who have similar issues. Or maybe you have some allies elsewhere in the organization who have seen what's going on, and you know they have verbalized some of their concerns to your boss's boss.

"Another senior colleague in the company knew my manager was a problem. She told me that she communicated to people at a more senior level and that she couldn't support my manager being considered for a promotion. She actually told the higher-ups: 'I have concerns about [so-and-so] and can't recommend her for the role in good conscience.' That made me feel so much better that someone well-connected was letting others know that there were issues. It also gave me more confidence to talk to my boss's boss when the moment presented itself."

So while I wouldn't say that you should *never* talk to your boss's boss, I do encourage you to tread carefully and analyze the situation to see if it will be a safe and fruitful avenue for you to pursue.

SHOULD YOU TALK TO YOUR BOSS DIRECTLY?

In dealing with malignant managers, it would certainly be ideal if you could help them see the negative impacts of their behavior, show them how an alternative approach would produce better outcomes, and influence them to change their difficult (or worse) behavior.

Depending on your status on the team, and your particular manager's openness, it may be possible to provide some feedback at the right moment that your manager can really hear.

But there are often reasons why trying this strategy just feels like it won't work. Perhaps you rightly fear your manager and their potential response. Perhaps you worry that you will only make matters worse. Perhaps it feels fruitless, like it just won't yield anything. Or worst of all, perhaps the situation has dragged you down so far that you somehow feel like you are powerless and at their mercy.

"I didn't have any sense of my own strength—a sense of myself—at that time. I believed I was stuck and didn't have choices and just had to suck it up and deal. Of course, looking back, I should have been able to say something, but I just didn't feel like I could."

Your circumstances are unique, and only *you* can determine whether it's worthwhile to pursue this strategy. *If you think there's no chance that you would ever try to broach a conversation with your manager, then feel free to skip to the next section and focus on what you can do within your own control to improve your situation.*

If you think, however, that you might like to explore the possibility of providing feedback to your manager, there are a few factors to consider before you do so.

First, *really* consider the type of manager you have. If they're a Humiliator, Hyper-Controller, or Conniver, it's highly unlikely that your feedback will have any impact. These types are likely fully aware of how they're managing and somehow think that their behavior is not just ok but is the right way to manage. Their approach is highly top-down, so they're not very interested in input from anyone, let alone their direct reports. You might see if there are ways to influence their behavior, only if you feel safe and confident enough. A tenured education administrator, for example, told me:

"On a survey about communication, I rated her a 7 and commented: 'You communicate exceptionally clearly, but why do you have to yell at me to communicate?' That was a risk . . . . I might have incurred more wrath, or she could have written me up for insubordination. My colleagues were shocked, asking me, 'You really did that?' But I knew she couldn't fire me and my record was good. I do think it ended up helping. She wasn't used to people like me standing up to her. I think I was able to chill a bit after I did that, and she became less confrontational."

An erratic Rollercoaster might be open to your ideas—on a good day, of course—but it's hard to predict what they will think about your feedback when their mood shifts. A Spotlight Snatcher, Work-Life Balance Breaker, or Neglector might be more likely candidates for feedback and change. There's a chance that they're not fully aware of how their behavior is affecting those they manage, and you might be able to provide specific suggestions that shift their patterns and facilitate some improvements.

"I have spoken to her a few times about how challenging it is when she repeatedly changes her mind about things. I explain that people feel whipsawed and can't perform. I think that I have been here long enough that she trusts my opinion, and I think she respects me for speaking up. Unfortunately, my feedback hasn't really changed her behavior yet, but I keep trying."

Another factor to consider is whether you've heard your manager ask for feedback, either directly from you or others on your team. If they've expressed openness before, there is a chance that feedback delivered in a constructive way will be heard. As you weigh the decision, you might also think about how you will feel if you *don't* try talking with your manager. Will you feel you've let yourself down somehow? Will your self-esteem take an additional hit if you don't make an attempt to stand up for yourself?

If you decide that you would like to try talking with your manager, it's worth taking the time first to think through exactly what you will say, when you might say it, and whether others could or should join you for this conversation. Helpful feedback should be as specific as possible, focusing on a situation that has happened recently, the impact it had on you, and your proposed alternative solution for next time. General, broad-brush statements about how your manager hasn't been helpful to you or about things they "always" do will make it hard for them to know what to do or say differently next time. Such generalities might also sound accusatory, which will put them on the defensive. So really take the time to think about a specific story or example you can share to make your point.

"I felt like I had to wait for the right moment to say something, and I was nervous as hell. But there was a specific incident that was easy to point to and explain how his behavior harmed a team member who is really essential to the team. He did hear me that time."

If you have multiple complaints, consider starting with just one specific issue to tackle. Perhaps it was a key one-on-one meeting with you that your manager canceled without offering to reschedule.

Or perhaps it was a meeting with higher-ups that you helped prepare for, but your manager didn't invite you or told you not to attend. Or perhaps they promised a client that you'd deliver something quickly without discussing with you first how long it might take. These kinds of specific scenarios might help your manager see what behavior would have worked better without raising their hackles.

In terms of when to offer this feedback, it's best to schedule a meeting when you know that your manager will be able to focus on what you're saying. A passing conversation in the hallway won't work. Asking for a meeting when you know your manager is under tremendous pressure is also not a good idea. Even if you're impatient for change, it pays to be patient and identify the optimal time for this kind of conversation. If your organization has a regular performance management process that includes discussion of next steps for your professional development, your performance review might be an ideal time for this kind of conversation. With a Neglector, for example, you can highlight how valuable the performance review meeting has been to you and push to schedule similar but shorter meetings once a month.

Another possibility is for you and a colleague to broach a conversation together. Especially if you both had a similar experience, like preparing for a big meeting and then not being invited by your Spotlight Snatcher to attend and present your work, you could both ask to discuss this with your manager. You would give each other moral support and a sense of solidarity and safety. Perhaps the feedback would be heeded because it's not only your word against the manager's.

Best case scenario, your manager will be receptive to your input and make changes. Try to be understanding if they don't completely change right away. As long as there's progress, that's a win. And your collaborative approach might set the stage for future discussions about how they can be more encouraging and supportive.

Your preparation for this kind of conversation should anticipate, however, that your feedback may not be well received or heard. You need to be prepared for negative responses, which could range from complete disregard, to defensiveness, to anger or retaliation. If it's complete disregard, well, then you're no worse off than before. But if their behavior toward you turns harsher, how will you respond to that? You want to think that through ahead of time.

For some of you, you may have to get to the point that you're ready to leave the organization if your feedback is poorly received. I have had some clients try talking to their managers as a kind of last-ditch effort to make things better. At that point, they felt they had nothing to lose . . . which was liberating.

"I was at my wit's end with the never-ending long hours and requests to work weekends. I could see that others were suffering, too. I finally said something about the pace not being sustainable. I said it nicely, but it didn't go well for me . . . She ended up using it against me and blocking my promotion. But I felt that I had to say something."

In the vast majority of my clients' situations, they have either tried to give feedback—to no avail—or were too afraid to try, feeling that such feedback could backfire completely. If this is your situation, then consider the other strategies in this section or the next one, so that you can navigate and survive until you land somewhere else.

Speaking of landing somewhere else, there will come a time—maybe not today, maybe not soon—when you are ready to start looking for a new job. Since it usually takes some time to make a move, the following chapter offers an additional set of strategies that you can use to begin that process. Sometimes just starting to get ready to leave can feel empowering and loosen the grip that your job and malignant manager have on your mind and spirit.

KEY TAKEAWAYS

1. Even if your work environment and manager are really harming you, it still might not be possible or desirable to start an active job search or quit. If this is the case, there are still a variety of strategies you can try to improve your situation.

2. Several strategies featured in this chapter focus on *you* and the steps you can take to help yourself. These ideas include: finding allies outside and inside the organization; writing CAR (challenge, action, result) stories to reconnect with what you've achieved; taking better care of yourself (for real); taking strategic time off; setting better boundaries with your manager; and even reframing the situation to see what you can learn and take with you.

3. Some strategies could involve other people, like HR representatives, your boss's boss, or even your boss directly. I urge you to tread very carefully. In many cases, none of these conversations are possible, but there may be some scenarios where they could be helpful.

4. However long you stay, choose the strategies that are best for you and your situation. Keep coming back to these ideas, as well as solutions that you or trusted family, friends, and colleagues identify, to make your life at work more tolerable and diminish the harmful impacts of your malignant manager.

IV

Strategies for Coping with a Malignant Manager— When You're Ready to Quit

At some point, it's just time to leave. You have suffered long enough, and it's clear that the situation at work is not going to get any better. Eventually, the pain of staying outweighs the discomfort of looking for something new. When you're ready to leave, then the challenges and questions are often practical. What do I do now? How do I go about it? This chapter offers a variety of strategies and tactics to make the process a bit smoother for you.

WORK ON YOUR EXIT, EVERY WEEK (NINE STRATEGIES)

Before getting into any specific strategies, let me say: Unless the situation is desperate, don't just quit! As you may remember from previous job transitions in your life, there's a lot of preparation that goes into a successful search. It could take some time. It's extremely rare that a new job just lands in your lap. Leaving before you have a new job can create issues, like financial stress, anxiety if the search goes on for a while, and gaps in your resume, which raise a red flag for some recruiters and employers.

It's best to plan, prepare, and work steadily toward an exit. This process can include at least the following nine specific strategies to get you ready, physically and emotionally, to move on to your next role.

1. *Identify target roles and organizations.*

Whenever you're looking for something new, it's critical to get as clear and specific as possible about what type of position you want next. Now, you may be thinking: "I just want to get out of here, and I'm open to whatever I can find!" And from your perspective, being open is good, because then more jobs will be available to you, right? But it turns out that openness is not helpful, because your whole search process will be unfocused and inefficient. The clearer you are, the easier it is to search for opportunities, prepare a strong resume and LinkedIn profile, and let people in your network know what you're looking for. If you're not sure what you want to target, it's worth taking some time to explore and discuss your options with trusted resources like friends, family, former colleagues, or a career coach. This time invested upfront will save you lots of unnecessary struggle later.

As you think about your next move, I must add that you don't have to change your entire career. Your manager may have beaten you down to the point that you are doubting your abilities, and you may be wondering whether you should do something else entirely. But based on my experience with many clients, I am confident in saying that the problem is not you or the career you've chosen—it's your boss. Underneath those negative thoughts and feelings you may be having right now, you are competent in your chosen career, and you likely just have to get back into a role and an environment where your skills and performance are appreciated once again.

2. Refresh your resume and LinkedIn profile to be more attractive for your target roles.

As soon as you start letting people know that you're thinking about a career move, many will ask to see your resume, and they may also check out your LinkedIn profile online. So, those materials need to be ready, positioning you for the direction you're heading and showcasing your qualifications for the kind of role you want. A benefit of refreshing your LinkedIn profile and aligning it with your target roles is that you may get more inbound inquiries from recruiters about open positions. Recent statistics show that 97 percent of recruiters and HR professionals are active on LinkedIn, looking for talent.[10] You might as well be part of that trend! If you're worried that your current manager might notice that you're updating your profile, you can choose your settings to ensure that no one gets notifications of your changes. You can also make subtle but still helpful content changes.

---

[10]Makai Macdonald,, "100 LinkedIn Statistics Every Professional Should Know in 2025," Product London, February 19, 2024, https://productlondondesign.com/linkedin-statistics.

Since you'll be on LinkedIn making changes to your profile's content, make an effort to be more active on the platform as well. For example, plan to add more connections every day, post updates and articles, comment on other people's posts, and so on. The more active you are, the higher you'll rank in recruiters' searches. Your posts will also help reinforce your expertise in your field.

Another added bonus of working on your materials is that the process of upgrading them may help you reconnect with your career track record, as discussed in the last chapter in the section called "Reconnect with What You Have Achieved." Just thinking through your experience, writing those CAR stories, and capturing your achievements may remind you that, despite the recent hits to your self-confidence, you really have valuable skills, experiences, and achievements to offer. One client told me:

"Doing my resume was a huge confidence boost. I realized that I am actually good at this work! The process pushed me to remember what I have done well. Now I have a better sense of how to talk about the good things I have achieved."

---

3. Network with friends, contacts, and former colleagues.

Even though there are countless online job boards out there with countless postings, the most effective strategy for finding a new opportunity is still networking. Starting to let your key contacts know that you're looking, and what you're looking for, lays important groundwork because they will, over time, be able to connect you with opportunities. If a job comes up that aligns with what you're looking for, they'll think of you. They may be able to refer you for jobs at their organizations or help you find an "in" somewhere else. Your network is one of your most powerful resources. Be sure to use it.

4. Explore internal opportunities.

If you work in a small organization, this option might not be feasible, but larger organizations usually provide opportunities for internal mobility. Think about where your talents might be useful. Are there other business units, departments, or teams that might have a need for someone like you? Are there projects that could use an extra set of hands? Can you set up informational conversations in other parts of the organization to learn more about what they are working on? Lateral moves can help you move out from under your malignant manager (at least for part of the time) and take a step toward work you really want to do.

"I networked constantly with others around the company, learning about what they do and occasionally asking if they had projects they needed help with. That ended up opening the door to a secondment in another department. I had to get approval from my boss, but it worked out. I got away from her, and that was my doorway to a new line of work too."

---

5. Start looking online and setting up job alerts for attractive opportunities.

Even though your odds of landing interviews can be low online (because many people apply for every opportunity and because applicant tracking software can screen out even the best candidates), it's still worth spending some energy online. The job boards can give you insights into the types of jobs out there and the expectations and keywords for those positions. Even if you're not ready to pursue a new job just yet, seeing the postings can help you mentally prepare as well. Setting up job alerts can ensure that you get relevant jobs delivered to your email inbox. And remember, if you see an opportunity with a particular organization, you might be able to find someone in your network who can connect you to the hiring manager or at least an internal contact.

6. Take recruiter calls and respond to inquiries.

There are a few reasons to take recruiters' calls, even if you're not ready to make a change or you don't think you're interested in the job. First of all, you never know: It may turn out that the role is a good match! But even if not, the conversations can give you valuable practice talking about yourself and what you're looking for. In addition, it's important to build connections with as many recruiters as possible. Failing to respond will never do that. Having a conversation gives you an opportunity to make a positive impression and assess how active they are in your field. It's very possible that you might want to contact them in the future, or vice versa. If you've built a connection, they'll be more likely to take your call or reach out to you when they're recruiting for a different role. Recommending other people to them is also a win-win; giving them names of others who might be qualified for the role both helps them out and creates positive goodwill, which might circle back to you down the road.

7. Start to prep for interviews.

This is easier said than done! If you've been dealing with a malignant manager for a while, it can be hard to believe in yourself, let alone sell yourself for a new role. I can't stress enough the importance of practice—specifically, talking about your qualifications for target roles, sharing what you've achieved, and doing so in a way that sounds confident. You also want to prepare for the inevitable question: Why are you leaving (or did you leave) your job? You want to be able to stay positive and avoid casting a negative light on your current manager or organization.

"I felt so angry about my boss and my company, and my emotions kept coming out when I talked about why I wanted to leave . . . I learned that I needed to start by highlighting some of the aspects of my job that I loved and all the things I'd learned. That set the right tone, and then I was able to share that I didn't see new opportunities for growth, so that's why I had started interviewing for new opportunities. That really worked!"

I'll share more ideas for dealing with this challenging question in a few pages. But there are many other interview responses to prepare to answer as well: "Tell me about yourself." "What are your top qualifications for this role?" "What are your key strengths and weaknesses?" "Why are you interested in this job?" Those are just for starters.

There are also "behavioral interview questions." These are the ones that begin with: "Can you give us an example of how you . . ." or, "Tell us about a time when you . . ." These questions demand CAR stories (see the "Reconnect with What You Have Achieved" section), in which you share specific examples of work you did, and the results and impact of that work. Sharing these stories can be very powerful in an interview, but telling them well takes practice. You can start your interview preparation by writing down your responses, but eventually you need to practice them out loud so that you can hear yourself. It's best to do this with a trusted friend, family member, or coach as well—someone who can give you feedback about how you're coming across and help you come up with better ways to say things, if necessary.

8. Line up your references.

At some point in the interview process, you'll likely be asked to provide references that your prospective employer can call. Under normal circumstances, your boss would be a key reference, but you may be thinking: "I could never give her name as a reference. She would definitely sabotage me!" So your goal is to figure out who in the organization can be an alternative. Ideally, you should find someone at a senior level, because your target company would value their perspective. Bosses from prior jobs should also be on your list. Make sure to contact these folks and let them know that you'd like to use them as a reference.

Note that you may have to explain to your target company that you're not including your current manager because of their erratic behavior. You want to say this as dispassionately as possible. Two pieces of good news about this: (1) By the time your prospective employer is thinking of checking references, you've already gotten to the point in the interview process when it's clear that they want to hire you. (2) They will understand! Almost everyone has had a horrible manager at some point. They will likely be fine with calling other people on your list; not providing your current manager as a reference will not be fatal.

9. Take a course to refresh your skills and potentially improve your marketability.

If your schedule allows, you may want to explore a course or certification (in person or online) that will enhance your qualifications for a new job. Even while you're suffering under a malignant manager, the experience of learning something new can give you a sense of positive investment in yourself and contribute to a feeling that there's a light at the end of your dark tunnel. Make sure it's highly relevant to your target role and will really enhance your profile for future employers. If you're lucky enough to work for an organization with tuition reimbursement, explore the possibility of using this benefit. This extra learning is for you; no malignant manager can ever take that away.

The key to working toward an exit is to do something on this front every week. It's easy to put off these kinds of activities if you don't plan to leave your job immediately. But as we all know, time gets away from us . . . Make sure to block off a slot or two on your calendar each week—even just 30 minutes—to make headway on one or more of these fronts, whether it's refreshing your materials, reaching out to a former colleague, setting up a job alert, or attending a webinar. If it helps you, set a deadline for completing some of these activities and find someone who will help keep you accountable to that deadline. You'll feel less mired in your current situation as you take active steps toward a change.

MAKE A FINANCIAL PLAN

Are you longing to quit your job but worried about your financial situation? If so, you're not alone. Concerns about loss of income and benefits are very real and can stymie your efforts to break free from a malignant manager. Often the questions include ones like: How long can I last without the income from this job? What if it takes me a while to find my next position? How can I be sure that I have enough financial cushion, so I won't feel pressure to take the first opportunity that comes up? You don't want to regret your move or—*gulp*—end up with another malignant manager! Financial constraints and worries are some of the reasons why I often encourage my clients to stay in their jobs and try to find a new one while they're still working.

But there may be good reasons to leave your job before you've lined up your next one. Your health may be suffering, for example, or your situation may be affecting your performance and you'd like to leave before it gets any worse. To figure out whether and when you have the financial means to leave, your best tool is a financial plan. If you have a partner or spouse, you should work on this plan together, so that you're both on board with your financial picture and the plan you develop. I'm not a financial planner, of course, so please seek out the counsel of someone who is. If you don't already have someone you work with, make sure to talk with someone who is a true financial planner and not just someone who can advise you on investments and insurance. Here are a few suggestions and thoughts (incorporating valuable input from a financial planner I trust):

Get a handle on your expenses. You'll want to really analyze your fixed expenses—the items you must pay every month, like rent, utilities, and car payments—and your variable expenses—the discretionary items that you can potentially reduce or eliminate, like dining out, new clothes, and streaming services. Examine your bills and payments over recent months. Many credit card companies also provide categorized quarterly or annual summaries that can help you see where your money is going. Where might you be able to cut back? Determine how much your monthly expenses would be if you reduced or eliminated some of the discretionary items.

Clarify your health insurance costs. If you're lucky, you can switch to your partner's employer for benefits, but that may not be an option for you. You may feel a bit stuck if you and your family are dependent on your job for health benefits. But there are some other possibilities. For example, you can keep your current health coverage through COBRA (a law that provides for continuation of health insurance), but you will be required to pay the full cost of the health insurance premiums.[11] That's a potentially big additional expense while you're not working, but you won't know if you can afford it until you find out the details. Alternatively, there are private insurance plans or, under the Affordable Care Act, you may be able to buy health insurance through a federal or state marketplace.[12] It will probably be worthwhile to do some research on the different plans that you may qualify for, as well as the costs and timeline for enrollment.

Carefully consider the timing of your departure. Depending on where you work and your level, you may be eligible for bonuses and stock or option distributions. There is a vesting schedule to consider when it comes to company stock and the employer match for your company retirement plan. If you can hang on, choose a date to leave after the next vesting, payouts, and/or distributions occur.

Shoot to create a fund that would cover at least six months of household expenses. Barring emergencies, this amount will give you some financial flexibility to search for a new opportunity. The number of months you choose can vary, of course. For example, if you're a very senior executive, you may feel that it will take longer than six months to transition into your next role. Or, perhaps you have additional savings in liquid investment accounts that you can fall back on if needed. Or, you may know that you're apt to become anxious without a larger cushion. Establish a number and a plan that are comfortable for *you*.

---

[11] "Continuation of Health Coverage (COBRA)," US Department of Labor, accessed June 1, 2025, https://www.dol.gov/general/topic/health-plans/cobra.

[12] "How to get insurance through the ACA Health Insurance Marketplace," USA.gov, accessed June 1, 2025, https://www.usa.gov/health-insurance-marketplace.

Don't dip into your 401(k) account or IRA, if you have one. In addition to the penalties that you will incur for early withdrawals, using retirement funds will also diminish your future nest egg. You may already be losing employer contributions to your retirement account when you leave. If at all possible, you don't want to compound the problem. Pretend these accounts don't exist. Build your plan around other resources.

There are surely other factors to consider that are unique to you and your situation, but hopefully these provide a few starting points for your financial planning efforts. If you are conscientious and deliberate, you can transform your worries about your finances into a plan, tamping down your fears and other emotions. You can avoid becoming desperate and give yourself a strong foundation for a positive and productive job search.

PREPARE TO EXPLAIN WHY YOU'RE LEAVING

As you think about starting to interview, one of the fears that may creep in is how you'll explain to a prospective employer why you're leaving your job. You don't want to disparage your boss, and you don't want to sound like someone who quits quickly or when the going gets tough. You also want to avoid getting emotional in the interview—conveying anger, frustration, or disappointment.

Obviously every situation is unique, but there are a few steps that anyone can take to prepare for this inevitable conversation. These include:

- Plan to talk first about the positives of the job and company, as well as highlights of some key things you've been able to accomplish (assuming you've been there long enough to have some results under your belt).

- Identify any logical reasons to leave the job that have little or nothing to do with your manager. For example, has the scope of your role changed? Has there been a restructuring? Is the company in turmoil? Have you been there a long time or completed a key project, and it would now be a reasonable time to tackle new challenges? Even if reasons like these might only be *part* of the story, they're still true and are valid reasons to share in an interview.

- Practice your answer with a trusted friend or coach so you can be sure that your answer sounds truthful and complete enough without being too wordy or emotional. (Sometimes an overly long answer can sound like you're trying to hide something.) Practicing can also help you get to a point where your answer sounds clear and matter-of-fact, basically devoid of emotion except excitement about your next role.

- Avoid using phrases like: "We didn't see eye-to-eye," or, "We came to a mutual understanding," or, "It just wasn't a fit," because you may risk having someone infer that there was something wrong with you or your performance.

"I really dreaded being asked why I was leaving my job. I was sure that they'd be able to read on my face that I was upset and embarrassed by my situation. Thankfully, the process of developing and then practicing an answer helped me get to the point of feeling ready, strong, and even able to say positive things about my job. I had to memorize and practice my answer quite a few times, but it felt so good not to have to worry about that anymore."

Remember that it's always possible to come up with a workable explanation for why you're leaving (or why you left). It may take a little effort to figure it out and practice the words so that they come out without anger or other emotions, but you *will* be able to do it. You won't be branded with some kind of "quitters' scarlet letter." People make career moves all the time, including to get away from malignant managers. Most wish they had done so sooner.

Hopefully all the ideas in the last two chapters offer you a sense of possibility and help you see that you can improve your current situation and move on when you're ready. But if you're still feeling afraid and stuck, that's totally understandable and ok for now. It may have only taken a short time for your experience with your malignant manager to weigh you down, but it could take a while to get to a place of feeling strong again. If you've been working for a malignant manager for many years, it could take even longer to regain your footing. The process of navigating and overcoming your situation is usually emotional. Be patient with yourself and, ideally, get the support you need to move through it and eventually beyond it.

No matter where you are in the process of coping and moving on, I urge you to remember: Your current experience, no matter how long you've been in it, is temporary. You will reconnect with a good job and a good manager in the future. You will get through this. You will find a way.

KEY TAKEAWAYS

1. When you're ready to make your exit, you need very practical strategies to start looking for a new position.
2. Many strategies featured in this chapter focus on job search readiness—everything from being clear about what you want, to preparing your resume and LinkedIn profile and putting together a networking plan, to navigating the world of online job search and interview preparation.
3. If you must quit before you have a new job, financial planning is critical.
4. Explaining to a prospective employer why you're leaving or why you left can be a knotty problem. Take the time to think this challenge through and develop a solid approach.

How to Avoid
Malignant Managers

As you think about pursuing and landing your next job opportunity, one question may emerge: "How do I avoid ending up with another horrible manager?" I've had a few clients who had more than one awful experience. They started to feel like they were magnets for these kinds of managers, like somehow, they were to blame.

It may be helpful to work with a therapist if you have had a series of self-destructive relationships in different walks of your life or if you're aware that your own behavior in past jobs may have contributed to your bad experience. But, based on my work with so many clients, it's likely just rotten luck that you ended up with a malignant manager, even if it happened more than once. If you look back on the process you went through to get your last job, there may even have been nothing you could do to prevent ending up with your manager. I've had many clients who got hired by one manager, only to end up with a different (unfortunately malignant) one after a restructuring or after the original boss left.

"At the end of my second week on the job, a major reorganization was announced. I lost two projects and two of the three people on my team. The woman who hired me, and who I was excited to work for, got moved to another group in the company. The guy who inherited my group had also been caught off guard, so I'm sure he was feeling anxious and insecure, which probably affected how he treated me. But no matter the reason for it, I ended up having to deal with his terrible behavior for the next couple of years."

I've also seen situations where the interview process was entirely pleasant with no red flags at all. Multiple clients were hired by folks they considered friends, only to discover later that they were horrific managers.

So, I urge you: Don't spend time blaming yourself and extensively analyzing past situations to see what you did wrong. Instead, there are four areas where you can focus your attention and energy now to improve your odds that it never happens again.

GET CLEAR ABOUT
WHAT YOU WANT & DESERVE

Whenever you undertake a job search, it's important to identify and establish the specific factors you are targeting. Things like job title, job responsibilities, industry sector, company size, length of commute, pay, and benefits will be critical in assessing a job opportunity, at least initially.

But there are other criteria to consider as well—those relating to the work environment and culture. Here's where it would be helpful to ask yourself a number of questions about what you want, and then really take the time to write down your answers. Writing them down gives you a tangible list of items to refer to later when you're considering an opportunity and especially when deciding whether to accept a job offer. You can incorporate these criteria into your interviews as well, asking questions that will give you insights into whether this particular environment and culture will be good for you. More on interview strategies in a few pages.

For now, here are some of those questions you can ask yourself (on your own or with support from a trusted friend, family member, or coach) before and during a job search:

- What am I looking for in a company or organizational culture?
- What kind of organizational mission do I want to align myself with?
- What kind of management style works for me?
- What do I need/want from my future manager?
- What sort of communication style do I want my manager to have?
- What is the frequency with which I like to receive feedback about my performance?
- What kind of team environment am I looking for? What do I want to hear future colleagues say about what it's like to work there?

Some of your initial responses to these questions might be, "I'd like anything but what I have now!" But I encourage you to think deeply about what you need to thrive at work, not just in reaction to your current or most recent experience, but also proactively.

Really dream about what would be good for you. Those aspects are what you want and deserve.

Once you've written down all of your desires, then I encourage you to prioritize them. Or if that's too challenging, put them in columns, such as "Must-Have," "Important," and "Nice-to-Have." Between target job factors (title, pay, etc.), target work environment, and culture characteristics, you might have quite a long list of wants. You might not ultimately be able to get absolutely everything, but if they're prioritized, then you'll have a clearer sense of your trade-offs. You'll consciously be able to choose what you can sacrifice, if necessary.

There's a spiritual belief called the Law of Attraction which, in essence, is based on the following principle: "Positive thoughts may bring positive results into a person's life, while negative thoughts bring the opposite."[13] Proponents believe that people's thoughts and emotions are energy and that "like attracts like." In other words, the energy of your thoughts will manifest your experience, so positive thoughts and emotions will attract positive outcomes. There are books and movies centered on this belief, such as *The Secret* by Rhonda Byrne. Whether or not you believe this, the process of gaining clarity about what you want will empower you. You'll enter the job search process and upcoming interviews from a place of strength and confidence; you know your priorities, you know what you're looking for, and you will find a better situation.

It may also be helpful to remember—and *believe*—that there are many fantastic managers out there. They invest in their people, provide helpful feedback, encourage development and growth, and

[13]Kimberly Dawn Neumann, "What Is the Law of Attraction? A Complete Guide," *Forbes.com*, Feb 20, 2024, https://www.forbes.com/health/mind/what-is-law-of-attraction-loa/.

genuinely care about those around them. I have worked with many managers and leaders who fit this description! There's no reason why you can't land in a positive and supportive environment with a manager like that.

RESEARCH

Once you start applying for jobs and getting calls for interviews, take the time to learn as much as you can about the organization and your potential future manager. I wish there were more resources to make this possible, but there are a few. Here's what you can do to learn more:

Check out the organization's website and/or careers page to see what it says about its values and culture. First of all, is there any information at all about its values? If so, do the statements appear to be well thought through and real? Or are they generic? Do they seem to translate to the expectations spelled out in the job posting? Does the language resonate with you?

If there is substantive language about the organization's values and culture, then chances are good that they are embedded in the expectations and norms of working there. They might even be woven into performance expectations of managers or the workforce as a whole. For example, if commitment to diversity, collaboration, people development, or treating others respectfully are core expressed values, then these values should align with company practices and expected management behaviors. These are signals to look for as you research a company, go through the interview process, and assess the likelihood that their managers will adhere to such values.

Examine employer reviews on websites like Glassdoor and Indeed. There are a few places on the internet where you can read reviews about what it's like to work at a particular company or organization. Sure, you have to read these reviews skeptically. Disgruntled former employees will be motivated to write a negative review, while those who had a positive experience might not think of writing one. But if you see patterns of comments that raise red flags, you can take these into consideration and potentially weave them into your interview questions. More on this in the next section.

Of course, even if the research turns up bad information, sometimes it's hard to trust or really believe what you read:

"When I went on Glassdoor, I could see that her reputation was notorious—not in a good way—but we were connected and she had helped me in the past. I thought, 'Maybe these are just complainers.' You don't think it's going to be the same for you. My significant other said, 'You know she's going to do the same to you,' but I didn't listen. It seemed like a good career move for me at the time."

You could also discover that some of your concerns seem to be non-issues.

"At first I was put off by the manager's odd behavior when he reached out to set up an interview—like, he texted and asked if I could interview with him right that minute. But when I read some company reviews online, they were all super positive, and many employees specifically spoke about how this manager supported them. It gave me some confidence that taking the job would be ok."

Either way, if there's information on one or more of these sites, you might be able to get some insights to inform your decision.

Check out the LinkedIn profile of your potential future manager. Do they have any recommendations from former direct reports? If so, you should see some indication of how their direct reports were developed, treated, and encouraged. Unfortunately, not everyone has recommendations on their LinkedIn pages . . . but if you're lucky, there might be some helpful nuggets there.

Some other information to look at on LinkedIn might include: (1) information they share about themselves in the About section, including their management style; (2) how long they have stayed in various positions (short stints could raise a red flag, or at least indicate something to ask about); and (3) posts they make about their work, their company, and their teams. Many people choose not to add much content to their profiles, and many post infrequently on LinkedIn, so you might not get much insight there, but it's something to explore. One of my former clients, an outstanding manager, posts about taking time to vacation and recharge, and he also posts frequently about his team, saying things like:

"I could not be more impressed with the caliber of the marketing organization I've had the good fortune to work with and to lead. Our unique human-first and high performing culture shines brightly in marketing around the world."

If you saw something like this, you might feel pretty good about the company and team you're interviewing to join!

Talk to people in your network about the company and the manager. Take a few moments to see if you know anyone (or know someone who knows someone) with current or past experience with the organization, and specifically with that manager. You can potentially use your LinkedIn network to find relevant connections. These people are gold mines for information on the organizational culture and ways of working.

"I called someone who'd worked there to get a sense of the climate. She told me that there is micromanagement at all levels and it's a toxic environment. But I was in an unhealthy state of mind so I wasn't thinking clearly . . . I remember thinking, 'Oh, I can handle that. It can't be as bad as where I am now.' I should have listened to her."

If you're pursuing an internal move (i.e., another position in the same organization but with a different manager), you should definitely be able to get some insider information on what it's like to work with your potential new manager, like this client:

"I spoke to someone I know and whose opinion I really respect. He knew the hiring manager for the role and said she was awful. He worked for her for a while, so I felt like he knew what he was talking about. It was hard to do, but I ended up withdrawing my application for that role. Later, as I learned more about that manager, I was relieved to realize that I'd dodged a bullet."

You can't take any one person's statements or opinions as gospel, but it's information that can be valuable to your process. You might also be able to find out if there has been a lot of turnover on that manager's team (a potential red flag!), and you might be able to gather other information about what it's like to work there, such as whether the team works insanely long hours. These kinds of research efforts should give you information that will help to reinforce or counterbalance whatever you hear during the interview process.

INTERVIEW STRATEGIES

Probably the most important thing you can do to minimize your chance of getting stuck with a malignant manager again is to use the interview process to gather information. The interview is a two-way street in which you're doing your best to sell yourself for the opportunity, and the interviewers are selling the organization, the job, and the team to you as well.

"I always used to worry about putting my best foot forward and trying to get an offer. Now that I've been burned, I'm a lot more careful to figure out if the job is the right fit for me."

How you approach the interview will vary a bit, depending on what round of the interview you're in. In the initial screening conversation (often with an internal HR recruiter) as well as in the first round of real interviews (which might be with the hiring manager or someone else on the team), your primary focus should be on selling yourself for the job. You're trying to convey that you're a great candidate with the experience and qualifications to do what is needed. Even when you have the opportunity to ask questions, your goal is to find out more about the job itself so you can ensure that you're a good match.

During these initial rounds, you probably won't have much, if any, opportunity to dig into the organizational culture, working environment, and management style. But you can still listen and look for signals. For example, how courteously are you treated as the interviews are being set up and scheduled? How kindly does the manager interact with the HR person or administrative assistant who might be setting up the interviews? How timely is everyone for their appointments with you? What do they say about other members of the team and/or the projects that people are working on?

Take note of whether everyone (including you) is treated with respect. Listen for hints of how it sounds to work there. For example, did anyone mention anything about working super late every night this week?

Your opportunity to gather deeper insights into the work environment and team culture comes if you're invited back for later rounds of interviewing. In these rounds, you'll likely meet with other members of the team and, perhaps, other stakeholders. By this point, the organization is pretty interested in you, and you have the prerogative to focus more on assessing whether this is the right place and the right job for *you*.

In addition to whatever questions you have about the job itself, here are a few questions that you could add to your arsenal when you're interviewing with the person who would be your manager:

- Why is this position open?
- How long was the last person in the role?
- How long have you managed this team?
- Please describe your management style.
- What are some of the things you do to promote collaboration on the team?
- How would you describe the team culture?

- What qualities are important to be successful on this team?
- What kind of person should *not* work here?
- How do the values on the organization's website show up in the organization on a day-to-day basis? (Be specific—highlight items that align with your core values.)
- How do you support professional growth and career development on the team?

Another creative interview strategy is to present a scenario to the manager and ask how they would handle it. For example:

- Say we're in a prospective client meeting. What role would you play and what role would I play in the meeting?
- If you and I are working together on a project, what will you be doing and what would you expect from me?
- When someone on the team completes an important task or project, how and when will they get feedback on how they did?

As you're hearing your prospective manager's answers to these questions, you want to listen not only to what they say but how they say it. Your "antennae" should be up! What are their facial expressions? What's their tone? Do they seem at all annoyed or puzzled by your questions, or do they seem eager to answer? Are they asking you any questions about what you're looking for?

Assuming this manager has more than one direct report, you will likely also have the opportunity to meet with some of your future peers. In these interviews, some of your questions can be:

- How long have you been on this team?
- How would you characterize [manager]'s style?

- What are some of the best things and some of the most challenging things about working on this team?
- Do you feel like you get positive and constructive feedback on a fairly regular basis?
- How does [manager] support your growth and career development?
- What are the typical working hours?
- How would you describe the team culture?
- What happens if somebody makes a mistake?
- If you could change something about the company or team culture, what would it be?
- Would you recommend this position to a friend?

The answers to these questions might be very telling. One client learned that only two people on an 11-person team had been there more than four or five months! But again, you'll want to listen not only to the content of their answers but also to their tone, facial expressions, and body language. Do they hesitate a lot in answering your questions, or do they seem eager to answer? Do they seem collaborative in their approach and interested in welcoming you to the team? Are they smiling? If they are enthusiastic about the team and the manager, that enthusiasm will come through in the words they use, their energy level, and their facial expressions and body language. One person heard a prospective colleague say: "We have the Ted Lasso of managers." If you didn't watch the show, Ted Lasso was a consistently positive, encouraging, authentic, and humble leader who got everyone to perform at the highest level, with joy in their hearts. It would be great to discover such a manager through the interview process!

Sometimes the interview process finishes quickly, after just one round. They're sure they want you, and they make you an offer! Even though this is flattering and exciting, you still can request the opportunity to ask the manager some additional questions and to talk with prospective peers to do your due diligence. If there's any hesitation in connecting you with peers, that's a red flag; perhaps the manager doesn't value their input or doesn't want you to hear from them . . . but you should have the opportunity to satisfy key questions before accepting an offer.

If you use the interview process to gather lots of information and insight, then you've done what you can to go into a new job with your eyes wide open. You may hear or learn some things that give you pause—things that might be red flags or alarm bells. Maybe these bits of information will save you from entering into another malignant manager situation.

Or, you may still decide to move forward and take the job, even despite the warning signs. You have to run your own calculation against the priorities you previously established about what you want and deserve. It's possible that this job opportunity will give you something important—access to a new organization, a new career path, a long-sought-after promotion . . . Or maybe you've been out of work for a while and feel that you *need* to take this opportunity, despite the red flags. The pressure to take a job when you're unemployed can be very intense. Or maybe your current manager is pretty awful, and you figure this new one can't be worse!

———————————

"There was a warning bell: Every person who took the role before me and tried to turn the team around—they all left. Three people had left the position in one year! But at the time, I chose not to notice. I was confident in my ability."

"I didn't see how horrible he was at the time. I had known him casually before, and he had the capacity to be very charming. I knew him just enough to be comfortable but not enough to see the warning signs. Had I known him better, though, I probably

still would have joined his team because I was getting away from way worse."

Ultimately, you'll balance the information you get from the interview process with the other factors influencing your decision about whether to take the job or not. But if you have taken conscious steps to make an informed decision, you can at least be confident that it was the best decision at the time.

"Even though I heard some things that I'm not super happy about, I think I may still opt to pursue the job, because it would really give me an important chance to try something new. As long as I can find out that she's not super toxic, I think I might be able to handle the situation."

TRUST YOUR GUT

In our data- and fact-driven world, sometimes we don't assign much value to that little voice inside that's trying to tell us something. But one regret I've heard from a number of clients who ended up with a malignant manager is that they should have trusted their gut instinct—their intuitive knowledge that something was wrong.

"An alarm rang inside my head, but I wanted to work at this place. I remember thinking to myself: 'Hmm, I don't know if she's going to be a good manager or not.' I should have listened to that."

"I really wish I had trusted my gut. I knew before taking the job that there was a vibe on that team that I had question marks about."

———————————

Sometimes, your inner voice can be positive, too:

———————————

"When I interviewed for a new role, I could tell intuitively that the manager would be someone who would be supportive, who I could ask for help, who I could work collaboratively with. I felt so confident about her—like a breath of fresh air. I took the job and it was so worth it."

———————————

So, even though it's not very scientific, this last strategy for avoiding malignant managers is to pay attention to those intuitions and feelings inside. You've already done your research, asked your questions, and gathered whatever data you could. This last way of evaluating the decision is using another one of your senses. It's not likely to steer you wrong.

I wrote this chapter because I deeply care about helping my clients move on from a rotten situation, break the cycle, and get to a new work environment where they can express their talents, feel a sense of possibility and growth, and (most of the time) enjoy the way they spend precious hours of their day. I know that it takes time to pause and reflect about what you want and deserve, energy to do research and due diligence, gumption to ask tough interview questions, and courage to trust your gut, but these are the keys to avoiding another land mine. Here's just one example:

"I finally found the right place. They have been receptive to change and all the ideas I've brought. They really liked what they saw and gave me a promotion after eight months. It's all good."

This is the kind of vision I hold for you, too.

KEY TAKEAWAYS

1. As you approach a job search, it's important to take proactive steps to avoid getting into another situation with another malignant manager. The first step is to be clear about what you want and deserve. There are a variety of questions you can ask yourself, and writing down your answers is critical.

2. When you get into the job search and interview process, there are tools you can use to research the company, the manager, and the team. Take advantage of those.

3. Once you get into the interview process, there are quite a few strategies you can employ and questions you can ask to discern what the manager is really like. Don't miss these face-to-face opportunities to get real information and insights.

4. Always trust your gut.

VI

After You've Left a Malignant Manager Behind—You Will Recover

Hard as it might be to imagine at this moment, there will come a day when you are no longer working for that malignant manager who has had such a devastating impact on your life. It is only after you've gotten out from under that terrible shadow that you can start to see clearly how the experience has distorted the way you think, the way you behave, and the very way you see yourself. You will come to realize things like:

- "Oh, I don't really need to leave this career completely."
- "I'm actually good at this kind of work."

- "I have skills that are valuable in the job market."
- "That person and that situation were truly damaging to my mental and physical health."
- "I don't deserve to be in that kind of culture and working environment."
- "I am not to blame."
- "Wow, there really are great managers out there!"

Your mind may not allow you to have these thoughts and realizations until you have some distance from the situation, but they will come. And at that point, in addition to starting to see the truth about what you experienced, you can begin to take stock of what happened and what lessons you can internalize as you move forward in your career.

Based on my experience with numerous clients, I'd suggest that one helpful step to take is to find someone safe with whom you can vent about everything that happened when you worked for that malignant manager. I can't tell you how many people told me how cathartic it was to just let it all out. You may have been sharing some of your experiences with family, friends, coworkers, and/or a therapist already, but you may need to further release whatever else has been bottled up. The emotions you felt while working with your malignant manager can plant some deep roots in your mind and your body, often for years, and it's critical to find ways to uproot those unhealthy feelings.

Telling the story can bring up some bad feelings, of course, but stuffing the memories inside won't allow them to dissipate—at least not as easily. When you talk about the experiences, you'll probably also get some renewed validation from whoever is listening that your manager was pretty horrible and you didn't deserve that treatment.

A NOTE ABOUT LASTING EFFECTS

Depending on how brutal your workplace experience was and how long you reported to your malignant manager, it's possible that it will take a while to release the negative effects on your mind and body. Intense and chronic stress can be traumatic for many people. Without getting into detailed medical diagnoses, there are many different types of trauma with no single definition and a wide range of effects, symptoms, and severity, all the way up to post-traumatic stress disorder (PTSD). Indeed, I have had more than one client tell me that they underwent treatment for PTSD after leaving their malignant (and usually abusive or humiliating) manager.

But *your* experience doesn't have to be horrific to be traumatic, and you may need professional help to move through and past the lingering effects. You may also have internalized some fears and learned behaviors when you felt unsafe at work. These behaviors helped protect you when you were dealing with your malignant manager, but as you move into new roles, they could hamper creativity, flow, relationships, and performance. Again, some professional assistance may be necessary to help you unlearn fear-driven habits and move forward in a healthier manner. There's no shame in asking for help, and in fact, it may be the key that unlocks future career fulfillment.

MOVING FORWARD

Whether you have already landed in your next position or not, it is worthwhile to take formal stock of what you learned from your prior experience so that you can consciously do things differently in the future. Some of these ideas have emerged in prior chapters, but here are recurring themes that I've heard among clients.

Commit to being a better manager yourself. Whether you're a manager now, or may become one in the future, having a malignant manager does provide a powerful example of what NOT to do and how NOT to behave with your own direct reports. Take copious mental (or actual) notes specifically on what your manager did that was so harmful, so that you can choose different behaviors in the future. This is also your opportunity to become a student of good management practices. There are countless great books on management (a small selection can be found in the *Appendix* of this book). There are also numerous courses of varying lengths that are available online or in person through reputable organizations. Take advantage of these resources to convert your commitment to being a good manager into a lasting reality.

Recalibrate work/life balance. Many of us invest a lot in our work. After all, we spend dozens of hours on the job every week and, to some degree, our identity can get caught up in what we do for a living. But having a malignant manager can be a wake-up call to develop and nurture an identity outside of work as well, to realize that you are more than your job title and your work. Don't get me wrong: I personally believe that work is extremely important. Doing good work gives me (and many of us) a sense of contribution, influence, impact, satisfaction, and meaning.

But it doesn't have to be the sole source of self-esteem or meaning in life. One silver lining of an awful work experience is that it can push us to create a richer life—one in which we choose to invest more energy and time in family, friendships, personal interests, community volunteering, hobbies, health and fitness, and other aspects of non-work life.

Shift from helplessness to empowerment. For many people, one of the most crippling things about working with a malignant manager is the constant and utterly frustrating feeling of helplessness. It feels like there's no way to change the situation, influence your manager's behavior, or get out from under the cloud of bad feelings you have about yourself, your work, and your environment. Moving on from that manager provides an opportunity for a reset—a chance to leave that sense of weakness, vulnerability, and even victimhood behind. It may take working with a therapist to build or reclaim a sense of strength and resilience. A key goal as you move forward with your career is to reconnect with your inner sense of power and agency, or perhaps to find it for the first time. How much control and power you have will, of course, vary according to your level and position, but you should never again feel weak and powerless at work.

Acknowledge what has ended. In his seminal book, *Transitions*, William Bridges highlights the importance of paying attention to what is ending or has ended, because the ending is really the first stage of a new beginning. He states: ". . . endings must be dealt with if we are to move on to whatever comes next with our lives. The new growth cannot take root on ground still covered with the old . . ."[14] While it's natural to want to get away from an awful situation as quickly as possible and forget about it, you may find it easier to leave it behind if you focus on acknowledging what is ending in some kind of formal way. Perhaps even a completion ritual (such as burning something or throwing something away) might be satisfying. Allow yourself to truly close the door on your past experience to improve your chances of a fresh start.

Give yourself time to heal. As mentioned above, venting and counseling can be very helpful methods to process your experience. But lasting shifts in perception, mental health, and physical health take time. You can't really rush through change and transition. If your circumstances allow, give yourself the gift of time off between jobs to take care of yourself so that you're truly ready to move forward in

---

[14]William Bridges, *Transitions: Making Sense of Life's Changes* (Perseus Books, 1980), 91.

a stronger way. There's no rule about how much time is necessary, so you'll have to feel that out, but be generous with yourself!

Be a resource for others. From where I sit, it's clear that there are innumerable malignant managers out there, and their impact is widespread. What this means is that many people are struggling on the job and perhaps quietly suffering, and some of them may be your friends or family members. Reach out to people in your circle and ask how things are going at work. Hopefully, their jobs are going along swimmingly, but don't be surprised if they're not. Because of your battle scars from your experiences with a malignant manager, you might be able to offer support and ideas that others cannot. The simple knowledge that you've experienced something similar and have gotten through it could be just the inspiration that someone needs to keep going, explore some of the strategies for coping and moving on (like those outlined in Chapters III and IV), and take action toward change. As much as you might want to bury your experience with your malignant manager deep into a memory archive, your willingness to reopen those memories, share your story, and support others could make a huge difference in their lives.

TURNING THE PAGE

A malignant manager can be a central antagonist in the story of your life. But their part in your story will probably only last for a chapter. With planning, determination, action, and probably some help from others, you will write the next chapters of your career. Eventually, the malignant manager will be relegated to a minor part—probably not forgotten, but no longer a central character.

And if you're lucky, you might someday look back with gratitude for their influence on the way your story unfolds. But for now, I celebrate you as you turn the page.

Appendix

SELECTED RESOURCES FOR YOU

This is just a starter list of potential resources that might be helpful as you contend with your work situation and/or explore a job transition. There are, of course, many other resources out there. I urge you to do good due diligence before you commit time or money. But do tap outside resources whenever possible. No one should have to navigate a malignant manager or a difficult career transition alone.

Coaching & Therapy

Career Thought Leaders: https://www.careerthoughtleaders.com/hireacoach (use "Job Seekers" section to find a coach)

International Coaching Federation:
- Find a coach: https://coachingfederation.org/get-coaching/coaching-for-me/

- Find a local chapter: https://coachingfederation.org/community-events/icf-chapters/chapter-map/

Psychology Today, Find a Therapist: https://www.psychologytoday.com/us

Company Research

Sites with company reviews, rankings, and insights (in alphabetical order):
- Comparably.com
- Culturama.is
- Fishbowlapp.com
- Glassdoor.com
- Sloanreview.mit.edu/culture500
- Teamblind.com
- Vault.com

Legal

EEOC (US Equal Employment Opportunity Commission): https://www.eeoc.gov/eeoc-legal-resources

EmploymentLawFirms.org: https://employmentlawfirms.org/how-to-choose-an-employment-lawyer/

National Employment Lawyers Association: nela.org

Financial

CFP: https://www.letsmakeaplan.org/getting-prepared

National Association of Personal Financial Advisors: https://www.napfa.org/

FINRA: https://www.finra.org/

Forbes: https://www.forbes.com/advisor/investing/how-to-choose-a-financial-advisor/

Nerd Wallet: https://www.nerdwallet.com/article/investing/how-to-choose-a-financial-advisor

Other Information Sites

End Workplace Abuse: endworkplaceabuse.com

Workplace Bullying Institute: Workplacebullying.org

SELECTED RESOURCES FOR MANAGERS

This is by no means an exhaustive list of resources for managers, but rather a small sampling of books, articles, and training programs endorsed by coaches or recommended by well-regarded leaders and authors. Consider this a start—just a small slice of the valuable array of resources out there. My goal with these lists is to offer information that could be particularly useful to new managers, because the transition from individual contributor to manager presents an especially good opportunity to learn important lessons and skills. Several of these resources will also be helpful for experienced managers. May you find some valuable information and ideas here.

Books *(presented alphabetically by author)*

Leadership and the One-Minute Manager, by Ken Blanchard

Be the Boss Everyone Wants to Work for: A Guide for New Leaders, by William Gentry

Emotional Intelligence, by Daniel Goleman

Welcome to Management: How to Grow from Top Performer to Excellent Leader, by Ryan Hawk

The First-Time Manager, by Jim McCormick, Loren Belker, Gary Topchik

Everyone Deserves a Great Manager: The 6 Critical Practices for Leading a Team, by Jeffrey Miller & Todd Davis

Bringing Up the Boss: Practical Lessons for New Managers, by Rachel Pacheco

Radical Candor: Be a Kick-Ass Boss without Losing Your Humanity, by Kim Scott

Fierce Conversations: Achieving Success at Work and in Life One Conversation at a Time, by Susan Scott

The No Asshole Rule: Building a Civilized Workplace and Surviving One That Isn't, by Robert Sutton

The Making of a Manager: What to Do When Everyone Looks to You, by Julie Zhuo

See also: Teambuilding.com—12 Best Books For New Managers To Read: https://teambuilding.com/blog/new-manager-books

Articles

HBR's 10 Must Reads for New Managers—a collection of Harvard Business Review articles written specifically for new managers and addressing an array of topics.

This collection includes:

- "Becoming the Boss," by Linda A. Hill

- "Leading the Team You Inherit," by Michael D. Watkins

- "Saving Your Rookie Managers from Themselves," by Carol A. Walker

- "Managing the High-Intensity Workplace," by Erin Reid and Lakshmi Ramarajan

- "Harnessing the Science of Persuasion," Robert B. Cialdini

- "What Makes a Leader?" by Daniel Goleman

- "The Authenticity Paradox," by Herminia Ibarra

- "Managing Your Boss," by John J. Gabarro and John P. Kotter

- "How Leaders Create and Use Networks," by Herminia Ibarra and Mark Lee Hunter

- "Management Time: Who's Got the Monkey?" by William Oncken, Jr., and Donald L. Wass

- "How Managers Become Leaders," by Michael D. Watkins.

Training Programs

Center for Creative Leadership—Frontline and New Manager Courses: https://www.ccl.org/leadership-challenges/new-manager-courses/

Intelligent.com—The 6 Best Online Leadership and Management Courses of 2025: https://www.intelligent.com/best-online-courses/leadership-and-management-courses/

Teambuilding.com—17 Best Management Training Programs: https://teambuilding.com/blog/management-training-programs

Bibliography

Alnawwar, Majd A., et al. "The Effect of Physical Activity on Sleep Quality and Sleep Disorder: A Systematic Review," *Cureus* 15, no. 8 (2023). https://doi.org/10.7759/cureus.43595.

The American College Dictionary. Random House, 1962.

Bridges, William. *Transitions: Making Sense of Life's Changes.* Perseus Books, 1980.

The Cleveland Clinic. "Yes, There Is Such a Thing as Stress Sickness." December 1, 2023. https://health.clevelandclinic.org/what-happens-when-your-immune-system-gets-stressed-out.

Dinesh, Shradha and Kim Parker. "More Than 4 in 10 U.S. Workers Don't Take All Their Paid Time Off." Pew Research Center. August 10, 2023. https://www.pewresearch.org/short-reads/2023/08/10/more-than-4-in-10-u-s-workers-dont-take-all-their-paid-time-off.

Equal Employment Opportunity Commission. "Retaliation." Accessed June 5, 2025. https://www.eeoc.gov/retaliation.

Holland, Christopher James, et al. "Exercise and Mental Health: A Vital Connection," *British Journal of Sports Medicine* 58, no. 13 (2024). https://bjsm.bmj.com/content/58/13/691.

Macdonald, Makai. "100 LinkedIn Statistics Every Professional Should Know in 2025." Product London. February 19, 2024. https://productlondondesign.com/linkedin-statistics/.

Mayo Clinic. "Chronic Stress Puts Your Health at Risk." August 1, 2023. https://www.mayoclinic.org/healthy-lifestyle/stress-management/in-depth/stress/art-20046037.

Merriam-Webster Dictionary. "malignant." Accessed February 25, 2025. https://www.merriam-webster.com/dictionary/malignant.

Neumann, Kimberly Dawn. "What Is the Law of Attraction? A Complete Guide." Forbes.com. February 20, 2024. https://www.forbes.com/health/mind/what-is-law-of-attraction-loa/.

Peter, Laurence J. and Raymond Hull. *The Peter Principle: Why Things Always Go Wrong.* William Morrow and Company, 1969.

USA.gov. "How to Get Insurance Through the ACA Health Insurance Marketplace." Accessed June 1, 2025. https://www.usa.gov/health-insurance-marketplace.

US Department of Labor. "Continuation of Health Coverage (COBRA)." Accessed June 1, 2025. https://www.dol.gov/general/topic/health-plans/cobra.

Webster's Third New International Dictionary. Merriam-Webster Incorporated, 1993.

Acknowledgments

First and foremost, thank you to the clients who shared your stories and whose experiences inspired this book. Many of you agreed to in-depth interviews, and your voices are woven through these pages. I won't reveal your names, but you know who you are! Even while sharing some very painful experiences, you also offered me your support and encouragement, and I'm grateful.

Next, thank you to my cohort in Publish Your Purpose's Getting Started for Authors program, including the program facilitators—Jenn Grace, Ellen Patnaude, and Brandi Lai—and my fellow authors—Connie Allaire, Chris Argos, Julia Bowen, Natalie Suppes, and Casey Tonnelly. Your twice-weekly presence, incisive feedback, and ongoing encouragement were absolutely what I needed to convert the ideas in my head into fingers on the keyboard and words on the page. Extra special thanks to Julia and Casey for our ongoing meetings and your sustained support for many months after the formal program ended. Your being there made all the difference.

Big thanks to Mark Cohen, Karen Herckis, Lisa Kohn, Tara Lovanio, Derek Mazzarella, Robyn McLeod, Cindy Shortt, and Rachel Yurdin for your valuable insights and contributions to the sections on human resources, financial planning, leadership resources, and trauma.

A few early readers helped me take the book to the next level of readiness for publication, and I am deeply grateful for your generous contribution of time both to read it and give me meaningful feedback. I'm looking at you Evan Alfandre, Victor Alfandre, Nicole Alger, Susan Feinberg, Jeanne Knight, Marcelle Rand, and Kathleen White!

The fact that my manuscript somehow transformed from a Word document to the complete book you're holding in your hands was due to the hard work and support of my team at Publish Your Purpose. Thank you to Jenn Grace, Alexander Loutsenko, Emily Ribeiro, Nelly Murariu, and especially Catherine Whiting, for your guidance, support, and hard work!

I was buoyed countless times through this process by a circle of women, especially when my doubts and fears crept in and threatened to sink the whole endeavor. Over these last couple of years, I thought about or talked to at least one of you every week, and your presence in my life gave me the extra boost I needed to keep going. My deep love and gratitude to: Jill Abrahamsen, Nicole Alger, Kirsten Archibald, Heidi Armster, Debbi Barer, Alison Bergum, Wendy English, Cristin Fitzpatrick, Lauren Haller, Helene Hawk, Jeanne Knight, Lucille Petringa, Sharon Pistilli, Marcelle Rand, Katie Wilson Rogers, Janet Rossi, Betsy Scheffel, Kiko Teed, Kathleen White, and Rachel Yurdin. Thank you all for being there for me in so many ways.

I feel very lucky to have a loving and supportive extended family (including family of choice), filled with some incredible people. Even if we didn't talk about the book much, you have always been a crucial foundation for my life. I'm thinking especially about my siblings, Joanne, Tom, Rick, Vicki, Paul, and Stacey; my uncle, aunt, and cousin, Bert, Bonnie, and Katarina; my soul mother and family, Cleofe, Betsy, Raymond, and Ben; my second parents, Susan and Harvey; my glorious nieces and nephews, Anna, Isaac, Tommy, Sonia, Joy, Alex, Noah, and Sarah; and my compassion warrior family, Ben, Katie, Henry, and Anna. I love you all so much!

Finally, Victor, Jason, and Evan: You nourish me on so many levels, and because of you, I wake up every day with deep gratitude and joy. Thank you for being a source of strength and for supporting and believing in me. My love for you is boundless.

About the Author

Cathy Alfandre's purpose is to facilitate positive change in her clients' work. She is a career coach and resume writer who provides practical support and partnership to those seeking greater career fulfillment. Her clients represent a wide range of sectors, functions, and levels, and they often come to her at a mid-career crossroads. Cathy supports them in finding their way and continuing successfully on their journey. As a coach, she offers assistance with career discovery, job search, interviewing, and on-the-job challenges, with a focus on facilitating forward momentum and tangible outcomes. As a writer, she relishes delivering exceptional career marketing materials that express her clients' unique value and buoy their confidence and results in the job market.

Prior to launching her business in 2003, Cathy had 15 years' experience in the private and public sectors, including as a strategic human resources consultant and people manager. She also worked for a number of years as a college and career transition coach for low-income and immigrant women at a community-based nonprofit organization.

Cathy earned master's degrees in business administration (MBA) and industrial and labor relations (MILR) from Cornell University and an undergraduate degree from Yale University. She also holds Certified Career Management Coach (CCMC), Certified Career Transition Coach (CCTC), Master Resume Writer (MRW), and Certified National Online Profile Expert (NCOPE) credentials.

An active volunteer in her community, Cathy lives in CT with her husband of 30+ years and her adorable and nutty dogs. Her two sons have left the nest but fly in her heart every day.

Learn more about Cathy at www.cathyalfandre.com or www.linkedin.com/in/cathyalfandre.

The B Corp Movement

Dear reader,

Thank you for reading this book and joining the Publish Your Purpose community! You are joining a special group of people who aim to make the world a better place.

What's Publish Your Purpose About?

Our mission is to elevate the voices often excluded from traditional publishing. We intentionally seek out authors and storytellers with diverse backgrounds, life experiences, and unique perspectives to publish books that will make an impact in the world.

Beyond our books, we are focused on tangible, action-based change. As a woman- and LGBTQ+-owned company, we are committed to reducing inequality, lowering levels of poverty, creating a healthier environment, building stronger communities, and creating high-quality jobs with dignity and purpose.

Certified

B Corporation

As a Certified B Corporation, we use business as a force for good. We join a community of mission-driven companies building a more equitable, inclusive, and sustainable global economy. B Corporations must meet high standards of transparency, social and environmental performance, and accountability as determined by the nonprofit B Lab. The certification process is rigorous and ongoing (with a recertification requirement every three years).

How Do We Do This?

We intentionally partner with socially and economically disadvantaged businesses that meet our sustainability goals. We embrace and encourage our authors and employee's differences in race, age, color, disability, ethnicity, family or marital status, gender identity or expression, language, national origin, physical and mental ability, political affiliation, religion, sexual orientation, socio-economic status, veteran status, and other characteristics that make them unique.

Community is at the heart of everything we do—from our writing and publishing programs to contributing to social enterprise nonprofits like reSET (https://www.resetco.org/) and our work in founding B Local Connecticut.

We are endlessly grateful to our authors, readers, and local community for being the driving force behind the equitable and sustainable world we are building together.

To connect with us online, or publish with us,
visit us at www.publishyourpurpose.com.

Elevating Your Voice,

Jenn T Grace

Jenn T. Grace
Founder, Publish Your Purpose

.

www.ingramcontent.com/pod-product-compliance
Lightning Source LLC
Chambersburg PA
CBHW050014090426
42734CB00020B/3259